ULRICH SCHLIEWEN

My
Aquarium

BARRON'S

CONTENTS

1 Characteristics of Fishes

2 Making Your Fishes Feel at Home

Water: The Element of Life

Starting Up the Aquarium

Care, Feeding, and Health

6

Aquarium and Habitat Profiles

Reproduction in the Aquarium

What to Do When There Are Problems

Appendix

1

Characteristics of Fishes

Fishes are fascinating creatures with very interesting behaviors. It's amazing how they adapt to the widest variety of environmental conditions!

Where and How Fishes Live

Taking proper care of an aquarium depends on successfully creating a substitute habitat for the fishes and plants. To that end the most important prerequisite is a knowledge of the requirements of both.

FISHES HAVE COLONIZED nearly all freshwater habitats in the world, from dark caves to high mountain lakes. But most of the favorite aquarium fishes come from a comparatively small number of habitats: rivers, brooks, lakes, swamps, and mangrove swamps in the tropics.

Living Spaces

Many aquarium fishes come from various well-planted still-water regions of fairly large and small bodies of running water, lakes, and swamps. Often thick stands of delicate, feathery water plants are present. Where these do not thrive, terrestrial plants hanging into the water provide hiding places for the fishes and food creatures. Many small brooks have a water depth of only a few inches (centimeters). In rocky streams with a strong current, many fishes either live sheltered from the current behind stones or are equipped with fins or mouths like suction cups that they use to cling to stones. Fairly large brooks and rivers contain many different habitats in which fishes find plenty to eat and protection from enemies that would eat them.

Especially in coves and in flood areas during the rainy season, a layer of fallen leaves often more than 18 inches ($\frac{1}{2}$-meter) deep covers the floor of the body of water, and it attracts many fishes. Rocky rapids or fairly deep areas with a sandy bottom and embedded stones or deadwood constitute alternative habitats with many hiding places. The large East African lakes, Malawi and Tanganyika, present their own habitats with endemic fish species that usually occur in no other place. The species from rocky and sandy biotopes and open water are good choices for aquariums.

Aquarium fishes are not always wild-caught but rather are commercially bred. This beautiful strain of the fighting fish does not occur in the wild.

The most beautiful aquariums usually are
the ones that reproduce the natural habitat
of their tropical inhabitants in the wild.

Finally, many species come from mangrove areas and brackish-water pools in transitional areas between freshwater and salt water. These habitats are similar to the still-water areas of larger rivers and weedy still-water areas, except that they contain swamp plants and other plants that tolerate salt water. Various habitats place very different demands on the shape, ecology, and behavior of fishes. Many adaptations to these conditions have developed over millions of years in these species. Each individual fish reaches the complete fulfillment of its specific way of living in accordance with typical adaptations and specializations. The specialists among them survive only within very narrow limits of living conditions, and the generalists prefer a broad spectrum. Many aquarium fishes that are recommended for beginners are generalists. Some species, including favorites such as the cardinal tetra (*Paracheirodon axelrodi*),

---

With their "suction fins," river loaches are highly adapted to strong currents.
▼

also need very particular water and environmental conditions in the aquarium. But both types are "success models" of evolution because they have been successfully established in their respective habitats over long periods of time.

Adaptation Means Survival

Which adaptations turn a fish species into a model of success?
Food: The most important adaptation for survival involves the means and the efficiency with which creatures find and process food; without adequate nutrition there is no chance of reproduction, the key to survival, and thus for evolutionary success. However paradoxical it may seem, the key to one type of success can be the ability to take advantage of many food possibilities in the wild. Flexible generalists are not specialized in obtaining a particular type of food.

So, for example, with fish species from the South American Rio Negro, from which many aquarium fishes are imported, it was ascertained that most of the several hundred species from this river contained not one but rather many different types of food particles in their stomachs. The alternative strategy, that is, specializing in a single type of food, can also be successful if it involves such factors as mouth and body shapes that allow access to a food source that is not available easily or at all to other species. For example, long-nosed fishes such as the elephant nose fish primarily extract nutritious insect larvae from tiny holes that are inaccessible to short-nosed fishes. This advantage can turn into a drawback, however, if these specialists have to compete with generalists for easily obtained food, which is often the case in an aquarium. While the generalists quickly gobble up everything, the specialists are involved in so much competition that they manage to get only a few bits of food and so must go hungry unless they are kept and fed

pay no further attention to them, species that care for their young have an advantage when quality is more important than quantity. They produce relatively few, but larger, eggs, from which larger fry hatch; the adults take care of them for a long time and protect them from being eaten by enemies. Most cichlids care for their young in this manner.

DID YOU KNOW THAT . . .

. . . many fishes have an electric sense?

Have you ever wondered how many fishes, including sharks, manage to hunt successfully in complete darkness? This is possible because many aquatic creatures produce weak electric fields through muscle movements. Sharks and other fishes can detect these electric fields with highly sensitive organs known as electroreceptors. However, some fishes, including certain catfishes, the black ghost knifefish, and the elephant nose fish, not only can perceive electric fields but also have the ability to create their own special electric charges. They use these electric charges to locate objects and sometimes even for communication. In other words, they converse, so to speak, electronically. In addition, each species can have its own electronic dialect.

separately. So success is always a question of the conditions for competition.
Reproduction: One further key to success is the ability to reproduce cleverly and successfully. Although most fish species scatter large numbers of fertilized eggs randomly in open water or deposit them in thick vegetation and

On the other hand, live-bearing tooth carps, including such fishes as Guppies and Swordtails, bypass the elaborate caring for eggs and fry and instead give birth to large, living fry that are independent immediately upon birth. Species that do not care for their young do have an advantage over brooders, though, in producing as many young as quickly as possible. Still only a few of these fry have any chance of survival since they are heavily hunted as prey fish by other species.

Fish Anatomy

Fish anatomy reflects the varied adaptations to life in the water.

Body shape: Body shape is directed toward stabilizing the fish's body in the water, which is a viscous medium in comparison with air, and to minimizing physical resistance in water. Body shape differs according to current conditions and the preferred region (bottom or open water) that the fish inhabits. Many freshwater fishes, such as Kissing Gouramis, which don't have to deal with particularly strong currents, exhibit the classic fish shape: flattened laterally and with a slightly rounded back. Fishes with a particularly high back, such as angelfishes, usually come from still-water regions. Fishes from rapidly flowing open water, such as the zebra fishes, display a compact, rounded body cross section. Bottom or surface fishes are flattened either on the bottom or the back. Of course, there are a number of exceptions that don't fit into these categories, such as the snakelike freshwater pipefishes, burrowing flatfishes, and puffers.

Scales: The bodies of most fishes are covered with scales, which are embedded in a fish's skin like roofing shingles. In combination with the inner bones, the scales provide the fish's body with substance and afford a certain level of protection against enemies. But not all fishes have scales; many are "naked," and still others have bony armor. The mucous membrane covering the entire fish is particularly sensitive, and it rubs off easily. It uses embedded protective molecules to perform the important function of defending against disease pathogens, and its elasticity reduces the resistance of the fish's body to the current.

Fins: These provide the fish's body with lateral stability in the water and act as propulsion organs for movement. In many fish species they are greatly enlarged (often in males) to make the fish creature more impressive in its courtship display. In still other species fins have evolved into organs of touch (e.g, in the Thick-lipped Gourami) or reproductive organs (e.g., in livebearing tooth carps). There are distinctions among dorsal, caudal, and anal

◀ *The sand craters of courting males of many East African cichlids are fascinating. They use wonderful nests to try to lure females into laying eggs.*

fins, as well as between the paired ventral and pectoral fins. Many fish lack some of these fins; others have several dorsal fins or an additional small fin, known as the fat fin, between the dorsal and tail fins.

Air bladder: This gas-filled organ lies in the rear of the abdominal cavity. The air bladder, with its adjustable buoyancy, allows the fish to remain at a consistent depth. Accordingly, fishes that live on the bottom often have no air bladder, or only an atrophied one, and so they can sink.

Gills: Fishes use gills to breathe oxygen dissolved in the water. Water rich in oxygen is guided into the gill tissues, which contain many blood vessels, by pulsations of the gill covers. Fishes from waters that are very deficient in oxygen, such as many labyrinth fishes and catfishes, often have developed additional respiratory organs that allow them to breathe oxygen as land creatures do.

Senses

The most important sense organs of fishes are their eyes, their distance-touch sense, and their senses of smell and taste. Most fishes can see colors well. Fishes with particularly large eyes are usually nocturnal or they inhabit murky depths. Under very dark conditions, such as in caves and crevices in rapids, the eyes often atrophy or are totally absent.

The sensory cells that specialize in scent and taste are located in noselike sensory hollows on the snout or often on the end of cutaneous and often muscular skin folds on the mouth, the "whiskers." In dark and murky waters fishes feel the habitat with the whiskers and thus form a taste and spatial impression of their surroundings. Most people don't know that fishes also have a sense of hearing and hear quite well, and that they can produce sounds. Fishes also possess specialized sensory organs with which they detect pressure waves, which travel especially well in water. Corresponding sensory cells are distributed along the lateral line or in the head region and constitute the fish's normal sense of distance-touch. Fishes that come from dark bodies of water or that are nocturnal often display greatly enlarged sensory pores in the head region. Most fish species can also use electroreceptors to perceive weak electric fields generated by muscle activity in all higher creatures. Some fish groups have perfected and adapted the electrical sense (see p. 9).

Behaviors

Fishes are commonly considered "dumb." But they are not. Many fishes exhibit remarkably varied expressions of life. They use a comprehensive repertory of communication possibilities and behaviors, which will be described here. You can find information about reproductive behavior in the chapter "Reproduction in the Aquarium" starting on p. 120.

◀ *Zebra cichlids, which care for their young, are among the most devoted caregivers. The contrasting markings warn potential enemies of their aggressive behavior.*

Schooling behavior: Most likely the idea that fishes are dumb comes from observations of their pronounced schooling behavior, in which many individuals come together in a highly coordinated, large group in which individual fishes seem to express no individual differences but rather submit to the anonymous will of the school. Schools serve to protect against predators, for it is difficult for predatory fishes to focus on a single fish and attack purposefully—the dizzying effect of dozens of fish bodies is too much for them. Most aquarium fishes are not really schooling fishes that spend their whole lives in a school. They assemble into schools only in (supposedly) dangerous situations, such as when a predator comes into the vicinity or when they are put into new surroundings, such as a new aquarium. However, many aquarium fishes are social and live together in loose groups, as do many tetras, barbs, and live-bearing tooth carps.

Territorial behavior: "My home is my castle" is the motto for fishes with strong territorial behavior and those that temporarily or permanently defend a territory. The vast majority of territorial species defend a territory only temporarily, for example, when it's time to start a family in the mating season and while a brooding territory is being established for raising their young. During this time many gobies and all cichlids defend a fairly small spot very aggressively against potential enemies or competitors of the same species that are searching for a brooding territory that's still unoccupied. At this stage there may be problems in the aquarium, for the previously peaceable species "suddenly" consider the whole aquarium their brooding territory. Many species are territorial throughout their lives, for example, when it comes to defending productive but restricted feeding places. At brooding time the feeding territory becomes a brooding territory, and it often expands. Many fishes emit sounds to announce their territorial demands, as they also do in their courtship displays. Depending on the species, these sounds are produced by various organs, such as by rubbing together the rays of fins.

Fighting behavior: The most impressive, and in the aquarium often the most consequential, behavior is fighting behavior, and many fishes fight to the bitter end in the aquarium. Under natural conditions the weaker promptly pulls back, and after an initial sizing up of strength and an imposing display, the fight is over. The continuous aggression displayed in the aquarium primarily toward males of the same species occurs because the weaker fish has no place to retreat from the field of view of the stronger one, and thus flight is not always possible. So the stronger fish is continually incited anew to pursue the weaker one, and the confrontation nearly always turns into a harmful fight.

Purchasing Fishes Responsibly

By owning fishes that may have been captured in the wild, all aquarists find themselves in the sensitive area of animal and natural conservation. Often aquarists are reproached with the accusation that a majority of aquarium fishes are not kept properly and that only a fraction of exporters and importers of wild fishes provide optimal transport and temporary holding conditions. Also, since there are some black sheep even among aquarists, ornamental fish exporters, importers, and pet shop owners, it is especially important that you be circumspect in buying and caring for your fishes.

▶ 1   **There may also be fights between species.** Here, two killifish males exhibit imposing behavior.

▶ 2   **Catfishes,** farlowella in this instance, scarcely appear to exhibit behaviors. This impression is deceiving because many catfishes are nocturnal, and they need nothing more than behavioral communication that often goes unnoticed.

Fishes learn through conditioned responses

Fishes can be trained. When a stimulus and a reward occur in the same context, fishes display natural behaviors, such as swimming to a specific location.

The start of the test:

Feed the fishes only after making a particular sound or movement that they can hear or see. Since most fishes hear well, you can signal with a whistle before feeding. After a few days you will see that all, or at least many, of your fishes will swim to the feeding area after you whistle, even when you give them no food.

My test results:

Note: Before purchasing fishes of any species, find out about their origin, care, and social behavior. Avail yourself of reliable scientific literature and the knowledge of a competent pet shop owner. Try to find out what experiences other aquarists have had. There are some good opportunities for this through local aquarium associations and on home pages and chat rooms on the Internet.

Competent advice: Buy fishes only in pet shops where there are competent salespeople. A good pet shop owner will, for example, ask you about the size of your aquarium and if you have had any previous experience.

No discounts: Don't buy from pet shops that offer discounts on living creatures. The low costs for the fishes are generally possible only because of inadequate standards in transport and holding for subsequent sale.

Fishes Caught in the Wild

So far there is no known freshwater fish whose continued existence is threatened by the aquarium trade. This doesn't mean that removing living wild creatures is always without problems. It should rather make it clear that the endangerment of individual fish species lies in the destruction of their habitats. Utilizing fishes captured in the wild from ecologically intact regions can even help nature, rather than harm it. One example of this is the cardinal tetra (*Paracheirodon axelrodi*). This favorite ornamental fish species is one of the fishes most commonly exported from the Rio Negro region in Brazil. The cardinals are laboriously caught by hand by indigenous fishermen using nets, sheltered temporarily in net cages, fed, and flown from the Amazon metropolis of Manaus straight to the importing countries. By buying a cardinal captured in the wild, you indirectly support the ecology of this rain forest area. The indigenous fishermen can catch cardinals only in unspoiled rain forest areas, so the existence of both the cardinals and the fishermen depends on an unspoiled rain forest. So special environmental protection projects involve the continuous use of cardinal tetra, and this entails fair payment to the fishermen. So it's best to stay away from discounted fish!

High-quality strains of the blue ram cichlid bred in captivity are often more robust than the ones caught in the wild.
▼

Making Your Fishes Feel at Home

When fishes are swimming around together in an aquarium,
displaying their natural behaviors and perhaps even reproducing,
these are signs that your fishes are healthy.

Setting Up an Aquarium Properly

The technical equipment, a setup oriented to the fishes' habitat, meticulous water care, the proper food, and proper compatibility among inhabitants are the most important requirements for the successful operation of an aquarium.

FOR A SMOOTHLY RUNNING aquarium, there are a few details about the technical possibilities and biological and chemical connections in the water habitat that are worth knowing.

Care Requirements

Depending on species-specific living conditions, every plant and animal species has fairly specialized requirements. Aquarium equipment and care must therefore be specifically adjusted to each type of creature. But many interrelations are general, so the following advice applies as a guideline for nearly all aquariums. Also, it makes sense to gather specific information about the animals that you would like to care for before you purchase and set up an aquarium. That's the only way you can put the general information for each symbiotic relationship to the best use. Many fishes live in schools, yet others don't. Many require room to swim, others need a large surface on the bottom of the aquarium, and so forth. There is detailed information about special types of aquariums starting on p. 72.

Types of Aquariums — A Tough Choice

Some pet shops offer aquarium tanks in a great many sizes, materials, and shapes.

All-glass aquariums: The best are all-glass aquariums with silicone caulking and no frame, which are sold in standard rectangular sizes from 12 to 100 inches (30–250 cm). The silicone cement is very durable because the rubber chemically bonds with the glass as if two pieces of glass have been fused together. In addition, the cement is resilient and buffers minor tension

Blue gouramis ▶ show off their wonderful colors when they receive the best of care. Still, these robust aquarium fishes are less demanding than some others, such as discus fish.

from small irregularities that otherwise would lead to broken glass. In addition to the standard rectangular tanks there are "panorama" shapes with angled front panes, delta shapes (a triangular base with an angled front) that fit well into corners, and six- or eight-sided tanks that are especially appropriate for setting up in the open. Aquariums with curved front panes are technically feasible and also very popular—but they are expensive to buy and maintain because they require elaborately constructed stands and covers. Aside from the standard sizes and shapes, you can also have an aquarium made to custom dimensions relatively inexpensively. That way you can either address the specific space and current requirements of individual fish species or tailor your aquarium to the design of your living space.

Acrylic aquariums: Today these are the only commercially available alternatives to all-glass aquariums. Acrylic aquariums can be produced in all imaginable curved shapes and are significantly lighter than glass aquariums. With acrylic aquariums, algae deposits must be removed with an acrylic glass scraper

in order to avoid scratching the panes. Although they are quite appealing visually, these tanks are more expensive than those made of glass.

Note: The most commonly purchased aquarium is the 24 inch (60 cm) model, for it doesn't take up much room and it can often be purchased as a complete set at a very reasonable price. Small aquariums, like larger tanks, can be appropriate habitats for small fish colonies, as long as the fishes are selected in accordance with the reduced dimensions of the tank. Among the hundreds of species sold as aquarium fishes in pet shops, the only ones that can be kept in small aquariums up to 16.5 gallons (60 l) are those that remain small and have no major territorial requirements (see p. 75).

Cover Glass

All tanks that don't have an aquarium hood or that are not to be operated uncovered (see Checklist, p. 26) need to have a cover glass; a precut cover glass can be used in such a way that, on the one hand, it allows for feeding and the passage of wires for the technical equipment, and on the other, leaves no open spaces that tempt fish to jump from the tank and meet a tragic ending on the living room rug.

Aquarium Stands

All aquariums must be supported by a stable stand, and between the glass structure and the stand they need a $\frac{1}{2}$-inch (1 cm) polystyrene underlay or what's known as an aquarium mat, in order to buffer small irregularities and provide thermal insulation. Water weighs more than 2 pounds per quart (1 kilogram per liter), so even smaller

TIP

Custom-made aquariums

If you decide on an aquarium made to measure, consider whether it makes sense to make allowances for partitions for a large-capacity in-tank filter, a heater, and built-in drains. Installed on the side or against the rear pane, these partitions accommodate the technical equipment when an inner backdrop is installed.

2 **Designer aquariums, such as this one,** are offered by various manu-facturers in aquarium shops; their appearance changes in accordance with current tastes.

1 **A high-quality 16.5 gallon (60 l) aquarium set** with a hood is compara-tively inexpensive.

3 **Special shapes** for par-ticular niche require-ments, such as this aquarium room divider, are marketed by reliable manufacturers.

tanks involve quite a lot of weight.

Whereas a standard tank measuring 24 × 12 × 12 inches (60 × 30 × 30 cm) has a gross volume of about 15 gallons (54 liters) and can weigh about 150–220 pounds (70–100 kg), an aquarium with a length of 60 inches (150 cm) weighs all of $\frac{1}{2}$-ton—and with stone decora-tions and gravel, even up to a ton. This weight is supported not only by the stand but also by the floor. So both of these components must have adequate carrying strength.

For the standard sizes, pet shops sell aquarium stands precisely matched to the weight of the tank. As alternatives, and for setting up aquariums with non-standard dimensions, you will need either a custom-made stand (make sure to specify the total weight it has to sup-port) or a strong homemade structure made of bricks, aerated concrete blocks, aluminum shelving, or rectangular wooden beams that have a stable, water-proof coating. For aquariums with a length greater than 4 feet (120 cm), the carrying capacity of your floor should be checked by a structural engineer.

Aquarium Equipment

Filtering the aquarium water keeps the concentrations of visible and invisible contaminants low. Heating the water is necessary for most fish species, and lighting contributes to lush plant growth.

AN EFFECTIVE aquarium filter must fulfill several functions simultaneously.

Filter Function

As a mechanical filter, it removes large and small particles of dirt from the aquarium and collects them in the filter. These particles must be removed from the water cycle of the aquarium by cleaning the filtering material regularly.

As a biological filter, it fulfills its most important function by using its filtering material to form a substrate for the introduction of the useful filter bacteria that are extremely important for every aquarium. These bacteria transform the harmful organic waste products dissolved in the water, fish excrement and leftover food, into less harmful dissolved substances (see p. 22). An important consideration is that the more filter material there is as a substrate for the bacteria, the better the filter can function as a "water purification plant." An aquarium filter thus works as a chemical filter when special chemical and physical filtering materials, such as peat, aquarium resin, activated charcoal, and zeolite, remove dissolved substances from the aquarium cycle or transform them into different, useful, or less harmful ones.

Note: Every normal aquarium filtering merely transforms substances; they still need to be removed from the aquarium cycle through regular partial water changes (see p. 57) and cleaning of the filter material.

Types of Filters

There are several types of filters available in shops; most are combined with a pump that moves the water through them. There is a distinction between motor- and air-driven inside filters and motor-driven outside filters, which are connected to the aquarium by tubes and thus take up no room in the aquarium. The filter type you select is ultimately a matter of taste, for the functioning of the filter simply involves the volume and the type of filter material relative to the flowthrough speed: If the water is pumped at high speed through a restricted volume, the filtering effect is less than with filters that operate slowly.

Very small aquariums: For nursery or quarantine tanks foam mat filters (Hamburger Matten Filters) have proven adequate; they can be driven either with air lifts or centrifugal pumps. A tightly fitting filter mat made from filter foam with large pores is installed to create a space in which the air siphon or the

▲

Large aquariums, such as this Malawi community tank, require technical equipment tailored to the size.

motor pump is suspended. If needed, the rear clean-water chamber can be fitted with additional filter materials in mesh pouches. The suction effect of the siphon or the pump pulls the aquarium water through, slowly passes it over the entire surface, and effectively filters it (because of the large volume of the filter and the slow flow speed). The filter is cleaned by vacuuming it with an aquarium hose and occasionally by completely removing the mat and washing it.

Aquariums up to 32 inches (80 cm) long: For the filter I recommend small motor-driven inside filters, "piggyback" outside filters, or—most conveniently—small outside canister filters. In any case, make sure that the selected model is equipped with various filter materials. Since you can't put too many fishes in small tanks, modest performance

levels are adequate, as specified for the various tank sizes on the filter packaging. With motor filters, be sure to avoid selecting a pump that's too strong, or choose a model with adjustable performance (at outflow!). A filter pump that turns over the aquarium contents two or three times every hour is adequate.

Large aquariums 39 inches (100 cm) and longer: Large canister-type outside filters and multiple-chambered inside filters have proven useful for most filtering needs. Both types of filters are operated by quiet centrifugal pumps and are distinguished by a large filter volume and the option of equipping them with different filter materials.

21

Mechanical prefilters are especially useful for outside canister filters; they catch the major dirt before it reaches the filter itself and significantly lengthen the time between cleanings. A prefilter can involve a foam cartridge slipped over the filter intake; it can be replaced frequently and inexpensively. Outside canister filters are also available in the form of a practical "thermofilter" in which a heating element is incorporated into the filter canister so that there is no need to find room in the aquarium for a heater.

Note: Centrifugal pumps have a single moving part, an impeller wheel, which is mounted on an axle and is responsible for moving the water. The durable ceramic axles are subject to wear and should be cleaned regularly according to the directions or replaced in the case of pumps that are becoming noisier. It thus makes sense to have some spare parts on hand.

Filter Materials

In addition to the correct size and the type of filter, the choice of filter materials plays an important role in the functioning of the filter.

Filter foam: The most widely used filter material is the usually blue filter pad, which is available with either large or small pores. Inside and outside motor filters are usually provided in fitted shapes. Otherwise the pad material is available in sheet form. It can be cut with a sharp knife to fit a specific filter; the shape should be cut a few millimeters larger than the inside diameter of the filter so that it stays in place. A fine-pored pad should be used in the filter only after a large one, for otherwise it will get plugged up quickly and won't be able to perform the biological filtering. Filter foam has a practically indefinite shelf life, and it can be used again after being washed.

Filter mesh: This is used loose or as mats merely as the first stage of filtering in the main filter or as a prefilter material. Since filter mesh is used mainly as mechanical filter material, it can be discarded after being washed out a few times, before it dissolves over time.

Unglazed ceramic beads: Of all substrates, this provides the greatest surface for accommodating filter bacteria per unit of volume. Although this material is quite expensive, it's worth it. A liter or two (depending on the size of the aquarium and the number of fishes) will ensure a high level of biological breakdown of dissolved organic waste

◀ *Small internal power filters (left) are adequate for cleaning small tanks; outside canister filters (right) are necessary for large tanks.*

products in all filters. Because its pores are fine, it should be used only after large-pored filter material, and it can be reused indefinitely.

Activated charcoal: This removes mainly substances with a high molecular weight, including medications, pesticides in tap water, or substances that give the aquarium water a brownish or greenish tinge. As a result, activated charcoal is used after putting a medication into the aquarium or clearing up an off-color. Activated charcoal is available as chunks, pellets, or specially layered filter sponges, and it is used in the aquarium for about a week as needed. Loose filter charcoal must be thoroughly rinsed before it's put into the filter cycle in mesh pockets. It is removed after use.

Zeolite: This is the term applied to certain natural rocks that are capable of removing dissolved organic waste products (ammonium, ammonia, nitrite, nitrate, phosphate) from the aquarium water by combining with them. With high amounts of the above-named substances, $3\frac{1}{2}$–18 ounces (100–500 g) of crushed zeolite per 28 gallons (100 liters) of aquarium water (follow the directions!) can provide quick help. But since it also removes plant nutrients, it should not be used in large amounts.

Note: The chemical and physical filter materials peat and ion-exchanging resins are not used as real filter materials but for changing the hardness and pH value of the water (see p. 40).

Air Supply

The outlet of the motor filter above the water surface usually provides adequate aeration; the movement of the water enriches it with oxygen. The aeration effect can be heightened with a diffuser; this is a small plastic piece mounted on the pump outlet near the water surface and swirls the water and air together. Alternatively, pump-operated air stones can be used. The air is pumped through the porous ceramic, plastic, or wooden block and emerges as fine, sparkling bubbles so that the air (including oxygen) can dissolve in the water on its way to the top. Air stones must occasionally be abraded or decalcified in vinegar in order to continue functioning.

In crowded tanks and as a reserve for particularly hot days, oxygen releasers are a good choice. They provide additional oxygen to the aquarium by using a special fluid (hydrogen peroxide), which slowly breaks down into pure, reactive oxygen and water. In addition, the oxygen from the oxygen releaser helps break down the waste products from the fishes into relatively harmless products more quickly, so it is particularly useful in the start-up phase, when the filter bacteria are not yet functioning properly.

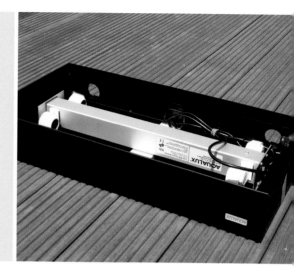

▶ **1** **Most aquarium lights** are fluorescent tubes inside a hood that's protected from splashing and cannot fall into the aquarium.

▶ **2** **Submersible heaters** (left) must be placed inside the aquarium or in the filter chamber, but flowthrough heaters (right) can be integrated into the cycle of the outside canister filter.

▶ **3** **Oxygen releasers** produce oxygen in a useful form without wires and distracting noise.

Heating

For normal usage, thermostatically regulated heaters are used exclusively; they can be set according to a temperature scale. The most convenient kind is a submersible heater with a glass jacket, which is placed inside the aquarium in an inconspicuous place with moving water or in a filter chamber. When you buy a heater, get one that's unbreakable and that has an overheat shutoff. Low-voltage bottom heaters can be installed as heating cables in the substrate. However, these cannot be tended to without completely cleaning out the aquarium.

The best method for heating a large aquarium involves an outside thermofilter (see p. 22), so that heaters don't need to be put inside the aquarium. The heating capacity is matched to the size of the tank and the outside temperature. The wattage shouldn't be too high, so that there are no quick temperature fluctuations. For a 16 gallon (60 l) tank at room temperature, I recommend 50 watts; for larger tanks the rule of thumb is $\frac{1}{2}$ watt per liter or quart. The functioning of the heater must be checked regularly with inside or outside aquarium thermometers, which are also available in digital models.

Lighting

For freshwater aquariums, either compact fluorescent tubes designated as T8 or the more efficient but also more expensive T5 tubes or metal halide lamps are used. They have a light spectrum that's suited to plants. There are also many lighting possibilities with various color components in their light spectrums, but a detailed description of them at this point is beyond the scope of this book. A good recommendation is to look for both good color reproduction and a well-balanced spectrum. A good reference point is the color temperatures specified in kelvins on the packaging. These should fall between 4000 and 6000 kelvins in order to produce a natural light that's good for plants. The various lighting devices require the appropriate holders and connections. In contrast to metal halide lamps, fluorescent bulbs can be integrated into cover lights. The lighting capacity of the bulbs should be increased with additional reflectors. Metal halide lamps, fluorescent bulbs, and combinations of the two must always be fitted with an integrated ultraviolet shield.

TIP

Small accessories

A properly functioning aquarium also needs two fish nets, an 8 foot (2.5 m) flexible hose, several $2\frac{1}{2}$ gallon (10 l) buckets or watering cans for changing the water, an algae magnet or a steel scraper for cleaning the glass, and an electric timer for turning the lighting on and off.

Setting Up an Aquarium

Setting up an aquarium involves mainly meeting the requirements of the fishes and plants. At the same time you can also create a beautiful visual picture for human observers.

AN AQUARIUM should display a perfect slice of underwater nature. It's really not too difficult to achieve this. The main consideration must always be the requirements of the inhabitants of this little underwater world.

Substrate

The basis of every aquarium is the substrate. It fulfills important functions for fishes and plants: It gives the plants food and a place to root; fishes use it in rummaging for food and creating hiding places; and the bacteria that break down harmful substances live in it.
Gravel: A good choice is a 2 to 3 inch (6 to 8 cm) layer of well washed (!) beige-colored quartz gravel with a granulation of 1–3 millimeters and no sharp edges. The best choice is riverbed gravel because it has already been polished round.
Note: If you want to use plants in your aquarium, the first time you set up your tank you should put in $\frac{1}{2}$ to 1 inch (1 to 2 cm) layer of a mixture of controlled-release fertilizer and the selected aquarium gravel to provide fertilizer over the long term. But set aside some areas in the aquarium without plants, where fishes, such as cichlids, will probably want to dig. If you have mostly fish that like to dig, these places or even the entire aquarium can use a thick layer of fairly dark quartz sand instead of gravel.
Sand: A sand substrate is essential for fishes that like to forage for food (e.g., corydoras, loaches), dig (e.g.,

CHECKLIST

Thinking ahead

Before you get into decorating the aquarium, make sure you have considered the following points:

- Which types of fishes need hiding places?

- Have you made plans for arranging the decorations?

- Is the substrate appropriate for all the inhabitants (sharp edges, lime content)?

- Have you thoroughly washed or rinsed the substrate and the decorations?

- In placing rock work, have you thought about measures to prevent stones from falling and breaking the aquarium glass?

"Nature aquariums" in the Japanese style look less natural but are esthetically more appealing.

lamprologus), or bury themselves (e.g., freshwater flounders).

Aquarium Backdrops

The assortment and arrangement of aquarium backdrops help create a sculptured, natural impression. The arrangement of the backdrop is not a decisive factor in creating proper living conditions for the fishes, however. Pet shops offer a wide assortment of attractive inside backdrops. They must be glued smoothly in place in the dry tank using aquarium silicone so that no fishes can get behind them and loosen them. Less esthetically discriminating are photo backdrops that are glued to the outside of the rear pane of the aquarium. A more relaxing effect can be created by painting the outside of the back wall with black or blue emulsion paint or gluing a piece of black roofing felt to the back of the aquarium.

Materials for Decoration

Setting up the interior of the aquarium with various decorations is keyed primarily to the needs of the fishes and plants.

Wood: The most important element in arrangements is natural-appearing wood. Aquarium shops offer wood items from a wide variety of sources; the best choices are Mopani and savannah wood. They don't need to be soaked, and they add practically no coloration to the water. Other types of wood that used to be sold fairly

1 Beech leaves collected dry and then soaked can be used to simulate an area of fallen leaves.

2 Nicely shaped roots provide shelter not only for individual fishes but also for entire schools of small fishes that feel more secure in the tangle of roots than in the open water.

3 Calcareous Karstic limestone is appropriate for Malawi, Tanganyika, and Central American tanks but not for soft-water tanks because of the lime content.

commonly, such as bogwood, moor oak, and what's known as mangrove wood, must be soaked for a long time so they don't float or give off pigments into the water. If you keep wood-eating Suckermouth Armored Catfish, you can also use naturally waterlogged deadwood from lakes and rivers; over time the catfish grate it up into small pieces, and this contributes to their appropriate living conditions. Since most wood gives off small amounts of acid-forming substances into the aquarium water, it should not be used in hard-water tanks with an alkaline pH (Malawi, Tanganyika, and Central America tanks).

Stones: Nearly all types of stones that contain no lime and have no sharp edges or shiny metallic inclusions can be used in the aquarium for constructing caves or entire rocky landscapes. The best choices are granite, porphyry, and slate in the form of gravel, chunks, and slabs. Stones containing lime such as dolomite are appropriate only for hard-water or brackish-water tanks. For safety's sake, before installing the substrate, place all fairly large rock structures on a thin polystyrene pad to avoid breaking the bottom glass. Carefully stack the stone structures so they don't wobble, and if you keep fairly large fishes, use silicone or special aquarium mortar to hold them together while they are still dry.

Hiding Places for Shelter

Many suckermouth armored catfish, cichlids, and gobies need caves to hide in. In addition to stone caves, you can use commercially made or homemade ceramic caves and pipes, bamboo tubes, or thoroughly cleaned, hollowed-out coconut shells.

Leaves: Did you know that many aquarium fishes spend nearly their entire lives under fallen leaves in the water? Forested areas at the water's edge provide a habitat for many aquarium fishes. The leaves that fall into the water provide food for insect larvae and crustaceans, as well as hiding and spawning places for such fishes as dwarf cichlids. A simulation in the aquarium can be

that you want to put into the aquarium. If it foams, it contains soluble carbonates. Decorative materials that contain carbonates are appropriate only for particularly hard-water tanks (Malawi, Tanganyika, and Central American tanks); otherwise, too much carbonate will be given off into the water.

DID YOU KNOW THAT . . .

. . . many fish habitats have no plants?

In deep oceans, on rocky shores, on sandy bottoms in calm water, and in dark jungle streams, conditions are often unfavorable for water plants. So an aquarium without water plants can be perfectly natural. However, water plants break down some of the harmful organic metabolic products in an aquarium. Well-planted aquariums often have very good water quality.

provided by gathering bunches of dry beech or oak leaves right from the tree in the late fall or winter. Before putting them in the tank the leaves need to be soaked for a couple of days. Put only a small amount of these leaves into the aquarium; otherwise they will upset the pH value and the water color, and the slowly decaying leaves will place the water under undue stress.

Note: Everything put into the aquarium should be free of carbonates. Check this using the "vinegar test." Put a few drops of vinegar onto a stone, for example,

Lush Plant Growth

Nearly all aquarium hobbyists want beautiful, lush plant growth in their aquariums. Not only is it attractive, but there is also another positive effect: The plants tie up contaminants in the water.

VARIOUS plant species often have different care requirements, just as individual fish species do.

Lighting for Plants

You can achieve the best lighting conditions for most plants by providing 12 hours of illumination with two or three fluorescent bulbs the same length as the tank, or with one 70-watt metal halide spotlight for about every 32 inches (80 cm) of tank length (with standard aquarium sizes). Plants that don't need as much light, such as many Cryptocorynes, Java moss, and Java fern, require less lighting intensity. It's important to know that the metabolism of aquatic

plants increases at a higher lighting intensity, so they also have greater nutritional needs.

Providing Nutrients

Good nutritional conditions result from a combination of controlled-release fertilizers in the substrate (for rooting plants), the regular addition of liquid fertilizers for aquatic plants (used very sparingly, according to the directions), and an adequate carbon dioxide (CO_2) supply (see below), which is necessary for a combination of hard water and demanding plants. In addition, trace elements such as iron must regularly be added in a form specially developed for aquariums because in contrast to many other nutrients, these are not available in sufficient quantities in tap water.

Carbon dioxide fertilizer: Carbon dioxide encourages strong plant growth. In order to add the right amount of carbon dioxide to the aquarium as plant fertilizer, you should know the relationship among carbon hardness, pH level, and CO_2 (see p. 134). This plant nutrient can be added to the aquarium water in various ways. In purchase and maintenance, economical devices use either fermentation processes, in which alcohol and CO_2 are produced from sugar with the help of yeast, or a harmless

---

TIP

Rhizomatous and floating plants

Strongly rooted plants need a sufficiently thick substraturn. Aquariums with digging fishes, and breeding and nursery tanks with a thin substraturn, can be lavishly decorated with rhizomatous plants, attached to waterlogged wood and floating plants and decorated in many shades of green.

---

chemical reaction in which CO_2 is produced (carbonation), as when effervescent powder comes into contact with water. Both of these types are appropriate for fairly small aquariums up to about 40 gallons (150 l). They have the advantage of simple usage without electricity, but they frequently need replenishing with newly purchased reagents. The more costly but more easily adjustable way to supply CO_2 fertilizer consists of a combination of pressurized CO_2 canisters, pressure-control valves, and electronically controlled dispensing, which is regulated to the pH level measured electronically. Those who can afford this should use it for fairly large aquariums; it is worth it, especially if they want to achieve strong plant growth under strong lighting. All systems should be checked, preferably with continuous pH-measuring devices.

Beautifully planted aquariums with strong lighting require additional fertilizing with aquatic plant fertilizer and carbon dioxide.

MY PET

Test for oxygen production in the aquarium

Under light, aquatic plants produce vitally important oxygen. The quantity of oxygen produced is generally related to the amount of light. You can test this relationship in the aquarium yourself.

Starting the test:

Take a little Crystalwort (*Riccia*) and use a cotton thread to tie it to a flat stone. Then place this stone with the Crystalwort into the aquarium under the area with the strongest lighting. When the lighting is turned on, you will see small gas bubbles form on the moss. This is pure oxygen, which is not produced in the dark. How long does it take for the first bubbles to form?

My test results:

Water Values

For most aquatic plants the water values are not crucial as long as the lighting and nutrient supply are in order and as long as neither extremely acidic nor very alkaline or hard water is used. But supplying the plant nutrient CO_2 is easiest in water with fairly low carbonate hardness. Water that's good for plants can be designated as water type 1 to 2 (pH 6.5–7, CH 1–6).

Recommended Plants

For starters, I recommend a small selection of plants that thrive and grow under a broad spectrum of conditions. These plants will provide a healthy aquarium environment for the fishes after only a few weeks. There is a distinction among rosette plants, which need a thick ground layer of medium-coarse gravel, rhizomatous plants, which are attached to stones or driftwood, and floating water plants, which grow as free-floating stems in the water or as specialized plants on the water surface. Bunch plants can be planted in the background of the tank.

EASY-TO-CARE-FOR
AQUARIUM PLANTS

Plant Name	Growth Form	Light Requirements	Water Type and Temperature	Size (cm)
African Water Fern *Bolbitis heudelotii*	Rhizomatous	Moderate	2–3, 75–77°F (24–25°C)	10–30
Schott *Anubias barteri* var. *nana*	Rhizomatous	Moderate	2–5, 72–79°F (22–26°C)	5–10
Amazon Sword Plant *Echinodorus bleherae*	Rosette	Moderate to average	2–5, 72–82°F (22–28°C)	30–60
Balansae *Cryptocoryne crispatula*	Rosette	Moderate	3–6, 68–79°F (20–26°C)	20–70
Needle Sagittaria *Sagittaria subulata*	Rosette	Average to high	3–6, 64–82°F (18–28°C)	5–10
Melon Sword Plant *Echinodorus osiris*	Rosette	Average to high	2–5, 64–82°F (18–26°C)	25–50
Uruguay Amazon Sword *Echinodorus uruguayensis*	Rosette	Average	2–5, 64–75°F (18–24°C)	50–70
Broad-leaf Water Sprite *Ceratopteris cornuta*	Floating Plant	Average	2–5, 72–82°F (22–28°C)	15–30
Water Wisteria *Hygrophila difformis*	Stem	Average to high	2–5, 75–82°F (24–28°C)	15–50
Water Hyssop *Bacopa monnieri*	Stem	Average	2–5, 64–82°F (18–28°C)	20–30
Creeping Red Ludwigia *Ludwigia repens*	Stem	Average	2–5, 72–79°F (22–26C°)	40–60
Najas conferta	Stem or water plant	Moderate to average	2–5, 72–82°F (22–28°C)	30
Water Sprite *Ceratopteris thalictroides*	Stem	Average	2–6, 72–82°F (22–28°C)	20–50

Wendtii Crypt or Tiny Crypt
Cryptocoryne wendtii

Type of growth/size: Rosette plant, 4 to rarely 12 inches (10–30 cm) tall
Water type: 2–5, 72–79°F (22–26°C)
Habitat: Sri Lanka, in shady or sunny flowing waters; doesn't need much light
Note: Belongs to the large genus *Cryptocoryne*, which includes many attractive aquarium plants; various requirements for water quality
Similar requirements: *C. beckettii, C. affinis*

Indian Swampweed (East Indian Hygrophila)
Hygrophila polysperma

Type of growth/size: Stem plant, 6–20 inches (15–50 cm)
Water type: 3–5, 72–82°F (22–28°C), thrives in hard water
Habitat: Indian subcontinent; needs lots of light
Note: Fast-growing stem plant that is ideally suited to planting around the edges of smaller tanks with fairly small fishes
Similar requirements: Pink-veined and small-leafed Indian Swampweed, *H. polysperma* 'Rosanervig' and *H. polysperma* 'Sri Lanka'

Tape Grass
Vallisneria spiralis

Type of growth/size: Rosette plant, 20–40 inches (50–100 cm) long
Water type: 4–6, 68–82°F (20–28°C), thrives in hard, alkaline water
Habitat: Europe and Southwest Asia, in still or slow waters; not very demanding in terms of light
Note: Robust, fast-growing plant for aquariums with hard water, in which other plants grow poorly; forms runners
Similar requirements: *V. Americana, V. nana*

Java Moss
Vesicularia dubyana

Type of growth/size: moss stem up to approximately 6 inches (15 cm), grows in cushion shape
Water type: 1–6, 59–86°F (15–30°C), adaptable to light and water quality
Habitat: Indonesia and the Philippines, on moist riverbanks, in shady places mainly on land
Note: Anchors to stones and roots; at first can be tied with cotton—later on it holds by itself; ideal plant for aquariums without substrate, moderate growth; can be trimmed with scissors

Java Fern
Microsorum pteropus

Type of growth/size: Individual leaves on a long rhizome; 4–12 inches (10–30 cm)
Water type: 2–4, 68–82°F (20–28°C), adaptable
Habitat: Tropical Asia, in shady, flowing waters
Note: Robust but slow-growing rhizomatous plant also for shady aquariums; tie rhizome to roots or stones with cotton thread; it will hold by itself; plant is usually left alone even by plant-eating fishes

Common Hornwort
Ceratophyllum demersum

Type of growth/size: Bunch or floating plant, 16–28 inches (40–70 cm)
Water type: 4–7, 72–82°F (22–28°C), likes hard, alkaline water
Habitat: Worldwide in various still waters depending on origin, various temperature requirements
Note: Extremely fast growing and undemanding as long as the water is not too soft and acidic; thus, better suited to breaking in aquariums or to improving the water in heavily populated tanks

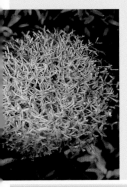

Crystalwort
Riccia fluitans

Type of growth/size: Cushion-forming, floating plant with loosely connected branched "leaves"
Water type: 2–5, 68–81°F (20–27°C), intolerant of current
Habitat: Worldwide in waters high in nutrients
Note: Forms thick cushions on the surface of the water, which may be used by labyrinth fishes for anchoring the foam nest. The photo nicely shows the finely branched structure of this fast-growing plant.

Brazilian Pennywort
Hydrocotyle leucocephala

Type of growth/size: Bunch plant, 12–20 inches (30–50 cm), sometimes longer, forms floating leaves
Water type: 2–5, 68–82°F (20–28°C), needs lots of light
Habitat: Latin America, in a wide variety of habitats
Note: Can be grown as both a rooted and a floating plant
Similar requirements: American Pennywort, *Hydrocotyle verticillata,* a species that should be kept cooler (63–73°F/17–23°C)

Water: The Element of Life

Water is just as important to fishes as the air we breathe is to us. Therefore, you need to devote all your attention to the water quality in the mini habitat of the aquarium.

Simplified Water Science

Whether the habitat in the aquarium is favorable or unfavorable for fishes and plants depends primarily on the composition of the water. The water quality determines whether the aquarium inhabitants thrive or decline.

AS A BASIC REQUIREMENT for understanding what goes on in the aquarium, you need to realize that the water is made up of a complex system. In other words, water is not composed of individual materials that can be removed or added without affecting other substances.

A Natural Water Purification System in the Aquarium

Two different groups of substances play an important role in the aquarium: substances resulting from the bacterial breakdown of organic waste products such as excrement and leftover food, which may stress the water, and groups of substances that consist of hardness-building salts and their chemically reactive partners in the aquarium water, that is, certain acids. Organic waste products (e.g., ammonium, ammonia, nitrite, nitrate) arise from the transformation of animal or plant material by specialized nitrifying bacteria. Many times other types of undesirable bacteria are already present in tap water in fairly high concentrations, and in this case they should be removed by using activated charcoal, zeolite, or reverse-osmosis water (see p. 42) before putting it into the aquarium. Normally nitrifying bacteria occur naturally in the aquarium, their growth sustained by decomposing leftover food, dead plants and animals, and fish urine and droppings. These raw ingredients are processed into end products in a natural breakdown sequence through bacterial activity. Like a water purification plant, the bacteria present in the aquarium use oxygen in a first step in converting the relatively nontoxic ammonium, which changes to poisonous ammonia in alkaline water (see p. 39).

Meticulous water care is especially important for breeding sensitive species such as siamese fighting fish (betta splendens).

In a further step, other bacteria process the ammonia into highly poisonous nitrite; however, with adequate bacteria in the aquarium, it is immediately converted to nitrate, which is poisonous only in fairly high concentrations. Nitrate in the aquarium is further processed only slightly or not at all, and it thus inevitably accumulates if it is not removed. In addition to these principal present in the aquarium. This is not the case with a newly set up aquarium, though. The highly poisonous ammonia and nitrite can quickly develop after the first feeding. To keep this from happening, after a new aquarium is set up, it must first be "broken in" (see p. 50).

Testing Water Quality

Aquarium shops sell test kits that use liquid reagents (droplet tests) to measure the concentration of individual

DID YOU KNOW THAT . . .

. . . many fishes live in extreme water conditions?

There are species of fish that not only survive but even reproduce successfully in extreme water conditions. One example of these is *Soda-Tilapia Oreochromis (Alcolapia) alcalicus*. It is found in the East African Soda Lakes, which can reach a pH above 10 and have water temperatures as high as 104°F (40°C) or more. On the other hand, there are many fish species that live in the black Amazon waters with extremely acidic pH levels below 4 and a mineral content that approaches that of distilled water. However, when caring for such extreme masters of the art of living it is not necessary to imitate these water values in the aquarium because what the fishes endure in their natural habitat is not necessarily what they ultimately need in an aquarium. Also, fish species that have adapted to extreme habitats thrive in a less extreme environment.

substances there are some waste products that are less critical to the fishes, such as phosphate and gelbstoff (residual organic matter). Phosphate accumulation can lead to unwanted algae growth. In order to achieve a functioning breakdown chain, there must always be an adequate number of bacteria organic waste products. The very user-friendly swab tests are just as good, but they go bad quickly and then become unusable (check the expiration date!). In the breaking-in phase of an aquarium, check the ammonium, nitrite, and nitrate levels daily. Later, every 1–2 weeks, or when you observe changes in

To keep your aquarium inhabitants healthy, the water quality in the aquarium must continually be checked and improved as necessary.

the fishes and plants, check the ammonium, nitrite, and nitrate, plus the phosphate content. Many aquarium shops offer the service of testing aquarium water. The following descriptions of corrective measures in cases of excessively high values are for emergencies, and they address only the symptoms and not the causes. It's important in the long term to (re)establish a functioning biological filtering system, or water initially free of harmful substances, perhaps through reverse osmosis (see p. 42).

Ammonium (NH_{4+}): This compound exists only temporarily in water with a pH level below 7, and even in high concentrations it is scarcely harmful. Thus the ammonium content doesn't necessarily have to be measured as long as you are sure that the pH level is below 7. But with a pH spike above 7 (e.g., because of a water change), ammonium turns into highly poisonous ammonia and can suddenly become a problem.

Ammonia (NH_3): This substance is highly poisonous, especially at concentrations above 0.05 mg/l. At excessively high values a radical 80 percent partial water change must be performed, possibly several times in succession. Lowering the pH level below 7 can also help, as can the immediate addition of fluids from the pet shop containing zeolite.

Nitrite (NO_2): This compound too is highly poisonous and should not be perceptible in a functioning aquarium. At excessively high levels a radical 80

percent partial water change must be performed, perhaps several times in succession. The immediate addition of fluids containing zeolite can also help.

Nitrate (NO_3): This substance is often present in tap water in concentrations up to 50 mg/l. Fishes can tolerate nitrate concentrations between 50 and 100 mg fairly easily; higher levels can be harmful over time, however. Excessively high levels are remedied through partial water changes with water low in nitrate compound or through zeolite filtering.

Phosphate (PO_{4+}): This compound is often present in tap water and should not exceed concentrations of 0.05 mg/l, otherwise it can lead to algae problems. Zeolite filtering helps at excessively high levels.

_____

This shell-dwelling Lamprologus multifasciatus cannot tolerate elevated nitrate levels in the water.
▼

In addition to the organic waste products, the interplay among hardening salts, carbonic acid, and the pH level in the aquarium is important.

Acidity/Alkalinity Level (pH): This value is an important one because many fishes and plants prefer either acidic (and soft) water and can't tolerate alkaline (hard) water over the long run, or vice versa. As with all other important values, you can measure the pH level with measuring tabs or fluid indicators from the pet shop. Depending on the acidity level, the water is designated acidic (pH level 1–6.9) or alkaline (pH level 7.1–14). Most fishes are most comfortable in slightly acidic to slightly alkaline water (pH level of about 6.5). But there are exceptions (see p. 38).

Water hardness: This describes the content of hardening salts in the water. Many fishes need not only acidic but also soft water. Water that contains few or no hardness builders, such as lime, is known as soft water. There are two important types of hardness: The most important one is carbonate hardness, which is measured in carbonate hardness degrees (°dKH), and the overall hardness, which is measured in degrees of German hardness (°dGH). The difference yields the noncarbonate hardness. Up to about 8 °dGH the water is designated as soft; at 8–16 °dGH, as medium-hard; and at all higher levels, as hard. The ideal water for most tropical river-dwelling fishes and plants scarcely contains any carbonate hardness builders (about 4 °dGH) and has an overall hardness of about 5–8 °dGH. The carbonate hardness, the content of carbonic acid dissolved in the water, and the acidity level are all directly tied in with one another. In the Active Test (next page) you can see how the values influence one another.

Conductivity: This value gives the overall content of dissolved substances (ions). In daily practice it's of only minor importance. It is measured electronically and recorded in mS/cm (microsiemens). Conductivity serves as an indirect measure of water hardness. The higher the conductance, the higher the probable hardness and salt content of the water.

Discus, like most aquarium fishes, like clean water.

MY PET

How to determine the pH value

The acid content in aquarium water is determined by acids and their counterparts, alkaline substances. You determine the acid level of the water by measuring the pH level. It depends on the relationships between these substances.

The test begins:

The effect of the most significant acids present in aquarium water is measured by the color change in the pH fluid indicators that you can buy. Take two glasses and drip liquid pH indicator into them. Use a straw to blow your breath, which contains carbon dioxide, into the glasses. A test made with carbonate hard tap water takes longer to move the pH into the acidic region (showing a color change) than one made with rainwater.

My test results:

Water Types

One can distinguish seven different water types in aquariums; they are a combination of carbonate hardness and pH level. I use these water types in this guidebook to quickly and easily indicate the underlying qualities of the aquariums described and the care requirements of the aquarium fishes.

Type 1: pH 4.5–6.5; °dKH 0–3
Type 2: pH 5.5–6.8; °dKH 3–8
Type 3: pH 6.8–7.5; °dKH 3–8
Type 4: pH 6.8–7.5; °dKH 8–16
Type 5: pH 7.2–8.5; °dKH > 12
Type 6: pH > 8; °dKH > 12
Type 7: pH > 8; °dKH > 12, with 3 teaspoons of added sea salt per 2½ gallons (10 l) of water

Water Conditioning

Depending on the region where you live, tap water may be adequate for your fishes. But if it contains harmful substances (high levels of pesticides, phosphates, or nitrates) or is hard, there is often no alternative but to mix the tap water with water that's free of harmful substances and hardness.

Reverse osmosis: With a small reverse-osmosis setup you can produce water that's free of both pesticides and hardness. At the same time, you will obtain three or four times as much leftover water, which is slightly more concentrated than tap water. This must be collected separately and can easily be used for other household purposes or discarded through the plumbing. Reverse-osmosis setups for aquarium use deliver between 8 and 40 gallons (30 and 150 liters) of water per day.

Rainwater: This water contains no hardness and can be used for mixing with tap water as long as it has not been contaminated by some inappropriate roofing surface (such as copper) or was not collected in a place with badly polluted air. It should always be collected after the first downpour and filtered for several days over activated charcoal for safety's sake.

Note: Mix bed demineralization of tap water using ion exchange resins is hardly worth the effort for aquariums because the exchange cartridges used in the process must be recharged at considerable expense.

Getting the Mixture Right

Since rainwater and reverse-osmosis water are nearly totally free of hardness builders and other salts (trace elements), you always have to mix them with tap water. The correct proportion between tap water and salt-free water is easy to calculate with the cross rule if you have determined the hardness (overall or carbonate hardness in °dGH or °dKH) of the tap water and know what degree of carbonate hardness or overall hardness you want to achieve.

Step 1: The degree of hardness of completely demineralized water (0 °dGH or °dKH) minus the desired degree of

2 **The most important water values,** pH, conductance, and temperature, are easy to measure electronically. Test kits that rely on color changes are economical if you are performing only a limited number of measurements.

1 **Crystal-clear** aquarium water requires intensive filtering—as in this large Malawi tank. Check the most important water values regularly.

The upper reaches of tropical mountain streams contain some of the purest water in the world. ▶

hardness yields the amount of tap water (without the minus sign).

Step 2: The degree of hardness of tap water minus the desired degree of hardness yields the amount of demineralized water.

Example: You want to produce aquarium water with 4 °dKH by mixing 16 °dKH tap water with completely desalinated water. According to the cross rule, you need to mix 4 parts tap water with 12 parts completely demineralized water (a ratio of 1:3). **Note:** The cross rule is not appropriate for determining pH.

Lowering pH Level (Acidifying) and Carbonate Hardness Reduction Using Peat

If you need only a little water low in carbonates or want to lower the pH level, you can do it naturally with fertilizer-free white peat granules from a pet shop. Put the granules into a gauze bag used specially for filter material and place it inside a canister filter, place it in one of the filter chambers of an inside filter, or attach it to an inside wall of the aquarium with a rust-free bracket. If you put it inside the filter, place a layer of foam filter material in front of the bag of peat. Measure the carbonate hardness and the pH level every day. Once the values are broken in or stop changing, remove the peat or replace it with a new supply. The used peat can no longer be used. Water filtered with peat is a clear tea color.

Hardening Aquarium Water

Sometimes it is necessary to harden tap water. You accomplish this by adding what's known as pH stabilizers or pH7/CH-plus reagents (follow the directions for use!) from the pet shop.

Starting Up
the Aquarium

Here's where things stand: You have selected a certain
aquarium, and now it's time to transform the dream of a small
underwater world into your own four walls.

Good Planning Guarantees Success

Where should the aquarium be set up? What do you need to consider in setting up the tank? How long does the break-in phase last? What do you have to be aware of when buying fishes and plants? You'll find the answers to these questions in this chapter.

AN "UNDERWATER LANDSCAPE" in the home requires a little advance planning. Various species of fishes and plants have different requirements, which must be taken into account. The right setup, the optimum running during break-in, the start-up of the aquarium and the technical equipment, and the proper acclimation of the selected fishes to their new habitat require planning so that everything goes smoothly. Of course, you should already know the best location for the aquarium.

The Right Location for the Aquarium

The aquarium inhabitants must be the major consideration in choosing the right location for the aquarium.

Load-bearing capacity: The load-bearing capacity of the room floor and the substructure play an important role (see p. 19).

Sunshine: Direct sunshine encourages undesirable algae growth. That's why the aquarium should never be placed on a windowsill or in an area that's flooded with sunlight.

Air circulation: The location for the aquarium should be well ventilated, for the fairly moist air surrounding the aquarium can quickly lead to the growth of mold on the wall. To play it safe, install a small fan in poorly ventilated areas.

Energy supply: Of course it is a big advantage if the wall sockets are located near the aquarium. That way you are spared from looking at long, unsightly extension cords.

Water connection: Especially with large aquariums, which require moving copious amounts of water for regular partial water changes, it's worthwhile to have a water supply and drain close enough for direct hose connections. This way

The distinctive iridescent coloration of the diamond tetra becomes visible when a little daylight shines through the side of the aquarium.

you avoid the hard labor of carrying water.

Quiet: Fishes need quiet, for they can suffer from stress. So locations with "through traffic," such as a hallway, are inappropriate.

Setting Up the Aquarium

In transporting and setting up the tank, make sure to avoid bumping it. Most glass is broken during transport rather than during the operation of the aquarium. Place thin polystyrene sheets or an insulating layer on the stand for the aquarium and put the tank on top. Use

Setting up: Above all, you should take your cues from the needs of the fishes you want to keep. This includes such things as the type of substrate, the preferred type of hiding places, the type of planting, and the availability of open swimming room. You can find out all you need to know by reading the relevant literature.

Required volume: How much controlled-release fertilizer ($\frac{3}{8}$–$\frac{3}{4}$ inches/1–2 cm) and substrate you need is determined by the volume of the aquarium (length × width × height in cm/1000 = number of liters of substrate). The volume requirement for

Too much commotion in the vicinity of the aquarium is stressful for the fishes. Therefore, be sure to put the aquarium in a quiet place.

a spirit level to be sure that the stand and the aquarium are exactly level. Make sure that the aquarium does not tip. Maintain a certain distance between the glass of the aquarium and the walls of the room to provide adequate air circulation and room for electrical cords and hoses.

Things to Consider Before Setting Up the Aquarium

Figure out what materials you need for the setup. On pp. 72–119 you will find detailed advice about some suggested tanks; you can it as a guideline for similar aquariums.

stones and roots is more difficult to figure out. It's better to supply slightly too much than slightly too little so you don't have to keep making improvements to the aquarium later on.

The need for water plants in the setup is commonly underestimated (see Tip, p. 30). When purchasing plants, stay away from plant assortments that have simply been thrown together. At first, select robust, fast-growing plants and obtain information about the requirements of any other plants you may want (see "Aquarium Plants" starting on p. 30).

1 **Before putting in any decorations,** install all life support equipment so you will have room later on to put in an inside backdrop. You may also want to reserve room for a heater.

In the second step the background is put up. Before adding **2** the substrate and controlled-release fertilizer, the heating cable on the bottom must be laid—if you are not using a rod-type heater.

3 **The planting** is done with only about one-third of the water in the tank. The plants are anchored in the substrate so that their roots are covered.

Then the prepared water is put in and the life support **4** equipment is started up. Be patient and wait about 2 weeks before putting in any fishes.

Setting Up and Breaking In

Now things get serious. Practice now follows theory. Set up the aquarium for its future residents and get it running. This is exciting and a tremendous amount of fun.

BEFORE YOU GET STARTED, consider that especially during the breaking-in stage an aquarium needs quiet. The efficiency of the aquarium mini ecosystem involves a complicated interplay among all the bacteria, animals, and plants in the aquarium that has to mature over the course of a few weeks. So the first attempt at setting it up has to "sit" so that later on you will have to deal with only a few adjustments, which are always a bother. Before the real setting up think about how you want to locate the individual elements. A sketch (see Tip below) can be very helpful.

TIP

Making a sketch

Before setting up the aquarium it's a good idea to draw a basic floor plan to scale showing where the stones, roots, decorations, and aquatic plants will be placed, and then cut them out. That way you can plan in advance for such issues as territorial borders for cichlids and structure them intentionally with the decorations.

Steps in Aquarium Setup

Now it's time for the individual setup steps (see photos, p. 47).

Step 1: If you want to put in an inside backdrop, cut it with a wood saw if needed. Attach the backdrop in the aquarium and glue it seamlessly with acetic acid-based aquarium silicone (don't use silicone made for plumbing and follow the directions for applying the silicone). After gluing, allow enough time for the silicone to cure properly. A 24-hour curing interval is prudent. After it hardens, rinse it with tap water and discard the rinse water.

Step 2: Now put in the life support equipment (filter, heater, CO_2 fertilizer, plus oxygen releaser and thermometer, if applicable) according to the directions in each case. Make sure the thermometer is not installed near the heater. The intake and outflow for the filter should be as far apart as possible so that the water circulates freely through the whole aquarium.

Step 3: Now the rock work can be added to the aquarium and individual rocks glued together, if desired. Put a thin polystyrene underlay beneath large stone structures. Stack up the stones securely and make sure they don't fall onto the glass bottom of the aquarium. You may want to secure the stone structures with silicone sealant; let it cure and then continue setting up the tank. Remove any excess polystyrene pieces because they can break off easily and float to the surface.

Step 4: Now put in the controlled release fertilizer (if desired) and the substrate in the appropriate thickness (see p. 26). Make sure that the substrate (not the fertilizer) is well-rinsed first.

Step 5: Now press the well-waterlogged roots or bogwood (see p. 28) into the selected locations on the substrate. Weight down any wood that may still float with flat stones, which you can later remove. If you want to put in some rhizomatous plants, fasten them to the wood with black cotton thread (because it's inconspicuous) tight enough so that the plant parts are well secured but without damaging them. Keep the plants moist in the meantime.

Step 6: Carefully fill the tank one-third full with lukewarm water (check the

For quick, strong plant growth, put in plenty of plants when you set up the new aquarium. Leave enough swimming room for fish that school.

water values). In so doing, direct the stream of water over a small bowl in the substrate so that the substrate doesn't swirl around and cloud the water too much.

Step 7: Put the rest of the plants into the substrate. Shorten any extremely long roots a little and carefully press

them into the substrate so that they cannot be further damaged. The substrate should go up to about the top of the roots, but no higher.

Step 8: Fill the aquarium with water; if you have to, replant any aquatic plants that float free.

Step 9: Start the aquarium up. Check and adjust the technical equipment.

Step 10: Now the break-in phase of the aquarium begins.

The Break-in Phase

In the first weeks after getting your aquarium set up and started, no fishes should be put in. The aquarium water is still more or less biologically dead because there are only a few bacteria in the aquarium and the filter. This means that no intermediate toxic products of organic metabolism (ammonia, nitrite) will be converted to the less harmful nitrite (see p. 39). Only after 2–4 weeks after setting will your aquarium be sufficiently biologically active, that is, the useful and essential bacterial strains will install themselves in the filter and the aquarium in quantities adequate for breaking down metabolic by-products. But the bacteria that produce the highly toxic nitrite grow more quickly than the ones that process the nitrite into the less harmful nitrate. Therefore, in the break-in phase at first there is a highly toxic accumulation of nitrite, which can be fatal to fishes. Only after 2–3 weeks, when daily water tests show no detectable nitrite in the aquarium, can the first fishes be introduced. A regular check of the nitrite level is also necessary shortly after putting the fishes in. The fishes raise the strain on the water, and the bacteria populations need to

▶ 1 **In the early stages** filamentous algae often grow in the aquarium. Amano Shrimp (*caridina japonica*) like to eat these algae and can be used for the purpose.

▶ 2 **Blue bristlenosed catfish,** much like siamese algae eaters, feed on algae. For proper living conditions, bristlenosed catfishes need wood roots and hiding places.

African moonyfish are brackish-water fishes. Brackish-water aquariums require a long conditioning period. ▷

keep growing. Regular partial water changes involving a one-quarter to a one-third of the water at intervals of 1–2 weeks are now required, for otherwise nitrate and other substances will accumulate.

There can easily be problems in the break-in phase or shortly after it, and they may also arise at other times, such as a major development of blue or string algae and cloudiness. You will find out how to react to such problems properly in the chapter "What to Do When There Are Problems," starting on p. 128.

Tips and Tricks for Reducing the Break-in Phase

Various methods will help you get through the break-in phase more safely and perhaps even more quickly. Here are some possibilities: Right from the start put in a fairly large quantity of fast-growing, robust water plants, such as Hornwort, *Najas conferta,* and Crystalwort. These plants at first take up a lot of metabolic by-products because of their tremendous growth and incorporate them into their vegetable matter.

The use of oxygen releasers helps in transforming poisonous metabolic products into less toxic ones.

Filter starter and previously used filter material from a broken-in filter establish bacteria concentrations right from the beginning and thus shorten the break-in phase.

Note: With all procedures that may shorten the break-in phase, it is important to check the water values at brief intervals in order to verify the true effectiveness of the methods.

51

Buying Fishes and Plants

You should take plenty of time in choosing and buying the future inhabitants of your aquarium. Make sure that the fishes offered for sale are really healthy and that the plants are strong. That way you will save yourself a lot of aggravation.

 BEFORE YOU GO to buy your fishes and plants, you should learn about the requirements of the preferred candidates for your aquarium.

Bred in Captivity or Caught in the Wild?

Many favorite ornamental fishes are bred in special breeding facilities for the aquarium trade. But many species can't be bred in an aquarium, or breeding them would be cost-prohibitive. Such species are captured in the wild.

In many cases wild fishes demand more care, but their colors often are more intense and vital than those of fishes produced by mass breeding. And yet high-quality fishes bred in captivity are in no way inferior to those captured in the wild. So the choice in purchasing should depend on the vitality of the fishes in the dealer's tank and not on whether they were bred in the wild or in captivity (see "Purchasing Fishes Responsibly," p. 14).

Where You Should Buy Your Fishes

There are several possibilities for purchasing fishes. The normal route leads to a qualified pet shop. Selecting the right pet shop is very important because you will get very different advice in different shops, and not every good small-mammal or bird expert is also a good fish specialist. It's best to get a recommendation from your local aquarium club or from a friend who has an aquarium. A good pet shop owner will take time and ask questions about your aquarium before selling you any specific fishes. But in case you are still uncertain about having received the

---

TIP

Sharing experiences

Aquarium clubs, as well as Internet chat rooms, offer the possibility of an intensive information exchange about keeping and raising even the most unusual fishes and plants. You should take advantage of this, for the collective experience of specialists cannot be replaced by a book, no matter how good it may be.

Capturing wild fishes for the aquarium trade is the livelihood of many people in the countries of origin.

right advice, a helpful alternative is to bring a good book on aquarium fishes with you when you go to the dealer. Check the descriptions of the care requirements of the individual fish species with the possibilities that you can offer in your aquarium at home. That way you avoid disappointments from the outset. You can also buy fishes on the Internet. Since this method is so far not widespread, you should make this type of purchase only on the recommendation of an aquarium owner who has already had a positive experience with the dealer in question. A good Internet dealer will also post proof of quality on the web page, such as certificates for the safe operation of the business and transportation from a veterinary standpoint. Finally, you can also get ornamental fishes from private breeders and from classified ads in newspapers. You may be able to find species that are rarely offered for sale in pet shops. As when dealing with a pet shop, you should form an on-site impression of the quality of the fishes and the aquariums before you decide to purchase.

Healthy Aquarium Fishes

Buy your fishes only from tanks in which
▸ ... there are no dead or dying fishes; other fishes may already be infected with the disease that killed the fishes;
▸ ... there are no fishes breathing heavily below the surface of the water, twitching, with fins stuck

◀ *This is how to equalize the temperature of the transport water and the water in the aquarium.*

▶ ... have their natural coloring; but as you evaluate them, remember that some fish species can act differently and that lying around calmly and a lack of color can be part of their normal behavior and appearance.

Transporting Fishes and Plants

Fishes and plants breathe oxygen and must be packed in a bag with oxygen gas (from the dealer) or air. Here are some things to consider:

▶ Use only bags with rounded corners so that the fish do not become entrapped in a corner.

▶ For transporting the fishes, fill the bag about one-third with water and two-thirds with air or oxygen.

▶ Put in the plants damp, but without much water and with air.

▶ Don't put too many fishes into one bag.

▶ Put aggressive fish species by themselves in smaller bags.

▶ Transport spiny fishes such as armored catfishes in a doubled, closed bag. Additionally, place a layer of newspaper between two bags just in case the first one gets pierced.

▶ For fairly long trips in the summer and winter, put the fishes in something like an insulated styrofoam cooler to avoid overheating or excessive cooling. Newspapers or insulated bags are adequate for short trips.

together, swimming in circles, or shying away from objects; these signs point to a poorly cared for tank or diseases that are already present;

▶ ... there are no fishes with white spots, cloudy eyes, or frayed fins; such characteristics are clear signs of disease (see p. 64);

▶ ... there is no yellowish, greenish, or bluish water; water that displays these colors points to the presence of medications and thus to diseases present in the tank.

Buy only fishes that

▶ ... look lively and act normally;

▶ ... have neither a distended belly nor an especially thin back musculature (knife back); poorly nourished fishes generally have short life spans;

Introducing the Fish

At home float the bag of fishes unopened on the top of the water in the aquarium and leave it there for at least a $\frac{1}{2}$ hour to equalize the temperature. To help the fishes get used to the new chemical levels in the water (since the water is slightly different in every aquarium), after a $\frac{1}{2}$ hour open the bag and carefully let in about one-quarter of the amount of the water in the bag. Repeat this procedure two more times at intervals of about 10 minutes.

Then let the fishes slide slowly out of the bag and into the aquarium along with the water or pour the water from the bag through a fish net and in a bucket and put the fishes in the aquarium without the water from the bag. Make sure no fishes get stuck in the corners of the bag or jump onto the floor as your pour out the water.

MY PET

Behavior of newly introduced fishes

Fishes placed in a new environment react with stress, for they don't yet know the potential dangers. When you introduce fishes to a new home, you thus get to observe the natural stress and orientation behavior of your fishes.

Observe the fishes:

After the fishes are put in the aquarium, solitary fishes will at first come together in a group if they don't immediately seek appropriate hiding places and bide their time a bit. Most species display typical fear coloration in this situation, which they lose when they feel secure. They also display this coloration as a result of faulty care or illness. What else can you observe?

My observations:

Care, Feeding, and Health

The right living conditions for the fishes, maintaining living
conditions in the aquarium environment, and healthy food for the
aquarium residents are the best ways to ensure the health of fishes.

Aquarium Care

There are three particularly important elements in the proper care of an aquarium: A daily check of the well-being of all aquarium inhabitants, the regular servicing of life support equipment, and regular water changes.

Partial Water Changes

Even the best filters merely encourage the bacterial transformation of acutely toxic metabolic products from the fishes into less toxic ones but without ultimately removing them from the aquarium (see p. 20). The best way to achieve clean water is to perform regular partial water changes involving one-fourth to one-third of the tank contents every week. That way you remove all the harmful substances dissolved in the water. Keep a hose handy, along with the appropriate attachment (e.g., a U-shaped tube that can be hung in the aquarium) and connections, that is long enough to direct the water to a drain and from the faucet or a container into the aquarium. Before changing the water, turn off all electric devices to keep the pumps and heaters from running dry. Then use the hose to suck out the water and the leftover food lying on the bottom. Pet shops sell hose attachments for this purpose that prevent inadvertently sucking up substrate or fishes. Then add water at room temperature and with the proper water values (see "Watering Can Method," p. 70).

Other Care Measures

Filter maintenance: After the filter break-in phase, which can take several weeks, only the first layer of the mechanical filter should be rinsed under cool water or replaced if it is falling apart or has become so clogged that it noticeably reduces the flow. The biological filtering materials should be rinsed only if the free flow does not function properly after cleaning the first filter stage.

Important: Never rinse the filter with hot water—that would kill the bacteria and interfere with the functioning of the filter. The temporary chemical and physical filter materials such as peat, activated charcoal, and zeolite wear out after a few weeks of use and must be replaced or regenerated.

Plant care: Regularly cut off leaves that are becoming yellowed or spotted,

Proper care for many Malawi cichlids involves principally proper feeding and good water quality.

Daily monitoring

The sooner you discover that something's not right in the aquarium, the less damage you will have to deal with.

○   If possible, observe all the fishes as you feed them. Watch for changes in behavior or appearance.

○   If you notice any changes, check the water values and for disease symptoms and isolate fishes that don't belong together.

○   Remove dead fishes from the aquarium before they contaminate the water excessively through their decomposition.

○   Carefully check the life support equipment and the water temperature.

prune and replant bunch plants, and illuminate water plants. Provide fertilizer regularly, but sparingly (the first time 4 weeks after setting up the aquarium), with special liquid fertilizers for aquatic plants. Use more controlled-release fertilizer only if growth drops off noticeably or if yellow leaves sprout. Cleaning the glass: Strong, floating algae magnets that remain in the aquarium are convenient to use. But these are not a good choice if you have sand on top of fine gravel in the aquarium because they catch grains of sand in the cleaning felt, which then scratch the glass. Instead, use plastic scrapers.

Maintaining life support equipment: With rotary impeller-driven pumps the ceramic shaft or the impeller wheel can wear or get dirty. If the pump is becoming noisier, the ceramic shaft and the impeller wheel must be cleaned according to directions, or if that doesn't help, they must be replaced.

Fluorescent bulbs and metal halide lamps change their light output so much after about 12 months that it may be worthwhile to replace them. But since some plants can't tolerate a complete change in light spectrum very well, you should not change all the lights in an aquarium at the same time but rather at intervals of a couple of months.

Sensors for the electronic measuring devices should be recalibrated according to the manufacturer's instructions to continue providing reliable readings.

Consumable materials for oxygen diffusers and CO_2-fertilizing devices must be refilled regularly to provide a consistent supply.

With reverse-osmosis devices you must change the fine filter regularly, and if the membrane is not used, it must be backwashed about once a week for a few minutes.

Food and Feeding

Providing your fishes with healthy food is no longer a problem nowadays. In pet shops you can find everything most aquarium fishes need for a balanced and varied diet.

IN THEIR NATURAL environment, tropical freshwater fishes have a broad variety of foods available. You can offer practically all types of fish healthy food: frozen, dry, gel, and live food available from pet shops. There are also a wide variety of special foods for certain fish groups with specialized dietary requirements. Some fish species won't accept any kind of prepared food because it doesn't move. For these fishes, and for the best and most varied feeding of all other species, you should raise some live food or buy it from your pet shop.

Look for Quality!

There are major differences in quality in both dry and frozen foods. Especially good-quality dry food consists of freeze-dried food animals; for fairly large fish it's also worthwhile to take a look at the food assortment in the terrarium department. But for beginning aquarium hobbyists this is not easy to figure out. So here's my recommendation: Get advice from experienced aquarists; they also share their knowledge on the Internet, which is easily accessible.

Note: Consult technical literature for the food requirements of individual fish species not included in the aquarium examples starting on p. 72 (see p. 142).

Dry Food

Dry food comes in the broadest array of compositions so that you can address the individual eating habits of specific fish species. For example, there are types that are rich in fiber for wood-eating armored catfishes, in green food for live-bearers and certain cichlids, and particularly nutritious nursery foods for young fishes. In addition, the food is available in various forms so that you can take into account the feeding behavior of individual species.

Flake food: This is the most common form of food for surface and midwater-swimming fishes, and it is accepted by nearly all species (at least after a short acclimation phase).

Fine or coarse granules: These are suitable for small or midwater water-living fishes and especially for bottom-dwelling fishes.

Pellets: Large pellets are especially appropriate for large, voracious fishes. But use any products for hatchery usage sparingly, for these are designed for quick growth rather than for the optimal health of aquarium fishes.

2 **Most fishes** love green food, such as blanched broccoli. To keep green food in place, it's best to attach it to a stone with a rubber band.

1 **Fan shrimp** (filter shrimp) are plankton filters. They display their natural behavior in the aquarium as long as they are offered a location with a moderate current.

3 **Food granules,** like other types of food, are a nutritious substitute for or a complement to the diet of most aquarium fishes.

Gel Food

Food in gel form is easy to divide up and is especially suited to bottom-dwelling fishes. Give it to fairly large fishes with the help of tweezers.

Food with Vegetable Supplements

Under natural conditions, most fish species, including true predators, are nearly always in search of food, and they spend the whole day eating small portions of food rich in fiber. So most fishes in an aquarium also need green foods rich in fiber. Many fishes, such as armored catfishes, like to nibble on fresh greens such as dandelion leaves, slices of zucchini, and chickweed. And you will find customers for occasional

green foods in many other aquarium fish species as well. It's a good idea to provide green foods from an organic food market. Try it to find out what your fishes like (see Test, p. 61).

Frozen and Live Foods

You can buy the broadest assortment of frozen and live foods in pet shops. You should keep a supply of deep-frozen live foods to provide variety and balanced nutrition and perhaps as a supplement to dry food. Since some fishes eat only live food, pet shops also offer a small selection of live food animals. But it's worthwhile to buy this food, which is heat-sealed in plastic bags, only if you need small quantities. If you need or want to offer your fishes live food over the long run, you should resort to the more economical culturing of Artemia Brine Shrimp, Grindal worms, or water fleas. You can get (Artemia) hatching kits and instructions from your pet shop, from ads in aquarium magazines, or from the Internet. You can buy the following from various suppliers of frozen or live foods.

Small shrimp: These food animals have a higher percentage of fiber than dry food. In addition, they contain natural pigments that intensify the coloration of fishes, especially red. There are various species of small crabs, and even the smallest ones are eagerly accepted by larger fishes.

Mussel Crabs, Bosmina, and Water Fleas: The nutritious mussel crabs (Cyclops) and Bosmina are highly recommended. Water fleas (Daphnia) contain fewer nutrients, so they are not suitable as a sole source of food.

MY PET

What kind of food do your fishes prefer?

Fishes have species-specific, and sometimes individual, food preferences that depend on what they ate in their "youth." You can determine your fishes' preferences through comparison tests.

The test begins:

Offer your fishes two types of food at the same time. The food type that they eat is the preferred one. At the next feeding offer the preferred food and a new type. This way you can find out the order of taste preference for individual fish species. It may happen that a particular food becomes "boring" and you get a different result after 6 months.

My test results:

An Aquarium for Children

Our two 8- and 10-year-old sons would like an aquarium with fishes and plants. We would like to grant this wish. But how would you approach this matter?

IT'S A LOT OF FUN getting children enthused about an aquarium. But since they have different capabilities for taking care of an aquarium based on their ages and characters, a children's aquarium should be as easy to care for and as stimulating as possible.

Fishes and plants that are easy to care for

Fishes and plants in an aquarium that are easy to care for must be able to tolerate minor mistakes in caregiving. There are species that by nature are accustomed to a broad spectrum of living conditions and have long proven themselves robust in aquariums. Such species are sometimes referred to as "beginner fish" and include such fishes as zebra fishes, platies, corydoras and catfishes, and blue bristlenosed catfishes. When such fishes are kept together with plants such as Java moss, common Hornwort, Wendtii Crypts, and *Vallisneria* in a large, well-lighted tank (28 gallons/100 liters and larger), the negative effects of errors in care are limited.

Providing motivation at the outset

Just like adults, children enjoy positive changes in the aquarium. Thus it's worthwhile to purchase accessories and fishes in stages, even if the aquarium is fully broken in. That way the living community builds up slowly and enthusiasm grows with new experiences. When this enthusiasm reaches a high point through reproduction of a species of fish that cares for its young, such as the bristlenosed catfish or mouthbrooding cichlids, it also serves for the sustained care for the aquarium. Naturally, depending on the children's ages, the parents need to remain involved in supervising this care.

Using the Internet as a stimulant

In my experience, it's great fun for children and their parents to look on the Internet for pictures and information about the fishes and plants that they have, their places of origin, and the habitats in which they live. Personal accounts of breeding fishes and pictures of healthy offspring also stimulate children to provide ongoing care. If a picture of the preferred species is installed as wallpaper on the desktop, the children are encouraged to provide successful care.

Mosquito Larvae: Among the various types of mosquito larvae, the smaller, black ones are a good choice, but small, white mosquito larvae are the best. You can also use an aquarium net to catch black mosquito larvae yourself in the summertime in puddles and rain barrels, where they hang right under the surface of the water. White mosquito larvae are sometimes sold live in pet shops. Both black and white mosquito larvae can be bought at any time in frozen form in pet shops. Bred red mosquito larvae, which you can buy in heat-sealed bags from pet shops, are great food for occasional use.

Note: Some people are highly allergic to red mosquito larvae!

Tubifex: One particularly nutritious food is what's known as tubifex worms, which are available live in shops. They shouldn't be fed to fishes too frequently because sometimes they contain high levels of toxins and lots of fat. For many fishes that are hard to feed, they are the right alternative if you can't get any

other kind of live food. Store tubifex worms in a container of water under a dripping faucet to keep the worms fresh.

Artemia Nauplii and grindal worms: Both types of food are easy to breed and help you get through the winter when there is not much live food available. If you decide to raise live food yourself, you will never have problems feeding any species of fish described in this book. You will find directions on raising *Artemia* nauplii from diapause eggs (cysts) in the chapter "Reproduction in the Aquarium" starting on p. 127.

Nutritious dry food can be adequate as a sole food source. But this applies only to undemanding species such as the platies pictured here.

Fish Diseases

If you have bought healthy fishes and taken into consideration the behavioral and care requirements of your aquarium inhabitants, not much can go wrong. Most diseases result from mistakes in providing care.

 FAIRLY ROBUST fish species can tolerate occasional, minor mistakes in care as long as they are promptly recognized and corrected. If not, the fishes' immune defenses will weaken, which often leads to a heightened susceptibility to infectious diseases or to poisoning. In rare cases introduced germs are the cause of a disease.

Poisoning

Poisoning by pesticides, chlorine, or heavy metals from tap water are often held responsible for insidious symptoms of poisoning in aquarium fishes. But poisoning can occur through errors in upkeep, which can lead to a gradual or sudden buildup of toxic metabolic substances, such as nitrites, ammonia, and nitrate, and be responsible for symptoms of illness in aquarium fishes.

Poisoning can be recognized by the following symptoms, which may appear individually or together.

Breathing problems: The fishes "hang" under the surface of the water, breathing heavily. Of course, this can be due to inadequate oxygen and also to the fact that because of poisoning the fishes' breathing is not working despite an adequate oxygen supply.

Fearfulness: Fishes are often seen to dart around inside the tank. They don't swim calmly but rather react with unaccustomed panic and jerky motions.

Noticeable pallor: Not only pallor but also excessively intense colors are indications of poisoning.

CHECKLIST

Stress factors

Stressed-out fishes easily become ill. The following factors can cause stress in fishes:

○ Too much commotion

○ Vibrations, for example, from tapping on the aquarium glass

○ Continually rearranging things in the aquarium

○ Harsh lighting in combination with a light-colored substrate

○ A lack of hiding places

○ An improper combination of fishes

○ Improper water values

In well-cared-for aquariums that are not too densely populated, there are rarely outbreaks of disease.

Note: Don't mistake suddenly intense colors for courtship coloration.

Apathy: Apathy is often combined with swaying motions in fishes; they are indicative of nervous system malfunction.

What you can do: Tap water poisoning from chlorine (swimming-pool scent) can be removed from the water by strong aeration (see p. 23). If you discover that the plumbing in your house contains copper or lead pipes, you should stop using water from this system in the aquarium. You can combat poisoning from the accumulation of metabolic products with massive partial water changes and filtering with zeolite (see pp. 57 and 133).

The Most Common Diseases

There are many different kinds of fish diseases. Most of them are described in the following.

Signs of disease: In general, sick fishes appear quite apathetic, often refuse to eat, and grab a food particle only to spit it back out. Fishes that have been sick for some time visibly lose weight and often cease displaying the colors they formerly had.

Fish Diseases
at a glance

Hole-in-the-Head Disease ▶

The causes of hole-in-the-head disease are not always clear, nor are there any certain cures for the condition. Often providing the fishes with food that's particularly rich in vitamins, adding trace elements to the water, reducing stress, and improving the water quality will help.

◀ Parasite Infestation

Rubbing against solid objects of the bottom of the tank is one sign of infection by an ectoparasite, that is, a parasite that freeloads primarily on the skin. These are often introduced on new fishes. You can get reliable remedies from the pet shop.

White Spot Disease (or Ich) ▲

This tetra has a case of white spot disease. The best way to recognize the first skin parasites is from a frontal angle. Treatment involves medications obtained from the pet shop.

Dropsy ▶

Bubble eye is usually caused by massive, untreatable infection from dropsy. The fishes usually become bloated, and the scales become ruffled. Such fishes must be humanely euthanized.

Prevention

The most important rules for preventing illness are the following: regular water changes and monitor water care; feed only the best possible food; and never buy any fishes from tanks that contain sick fishes.

White Spot Disease (or Ich)

Symptoms: White spots up to 1.5 mm on the upper surface of the body, heavy breathing, plus frequent rubbing.
Cause: *Ichthyopthirius* is a single-cell skin parasite.
Treatment: Various very good medications with a malachite green oxalate base are available in pet shops. Follow the directions carefully; otherwise there will be another outbreak. Avoid medications containing copper.

Velvet Disease or *Oodinium*

Symptoms: A whitish, gray, or golden layer of minute spots that looks like dust (individual spots are only 0.3 mm) appearing first on the fins and later on the entire body. The fishes frequently rub against solid objects.

Gill and Skin Worms

Symptoms: Fishes rub frequently, breathe heavily, and continually gulp without taking in food.
Cause: Parasitic worms on the gills.
Treatment: Use specially formulated gill and skin worm medications available from pet shops according to the manufacturer's directions or use brief Formalin baths under the direction of a veterinarian.

Dropsy

Symptoms: Unnaturally distended stomach and/or protruding bubble eyes and/or scales protruding like pinecones and/or humpback.
Cause: Infection by several kinds of mycobacteria.
Treatment: Incurable. Euthanize all afflicted fish humanely (see p. 69). The

Carefully inspect your fishes every day.
The earlier you identify a disease, the better the chances
of curing the infected fish.

Cause: *Oodinium* is also a one-celled skin parasite.
Treatment: Treatment should take place in fairly hard water with special medication purchased from the pet shop. In soft-water tanks, add common salt (2–4 teaspoonfuls of iodized salt free of other additives per $2\frac{1}{2}$ gallons/10 liters of water). When the disease abates, perform several partial water changes to avoid stressing the fishes and plants unnecessarily.

pathogen may remain in the aquarium water, but with improved care and living conditions the disease will not recur. If all the fishes are infected, euthanize them all, discard all gravel and plants, and disinfect the aquarium and all life support equipment with a tuberculosis disinfectant obtained from the pharmacy.
Note: Be sure to wear rubber gloves because dropsy can cause relatively harmless but very persistent skin

diseases in people. Consult a doctor if you experience changes in the skin of your hands.

Hole-in-the-Head Disease

Symptoms: Hollow depressions that slowly increase in size appear in the head region, especially with cichlids, such as discus fishes, native to waters that are deficient in minerals. The hollows may contain a white layer, but not necessarily.
Cause: Poor water quality (elevated nitrate levels), a lack of either vitamin D or calcium, or infection by single-cell intestinal parasites *(Hexamita)*. A combination of several factors may also be involved.

Treatment: First try enriching the food with special preparations you can get from the terrarium department, which contain vitamin D and calcium. If that doesn't help and the fish's droppings are stringy and whitish, you should get advice from a vet.

Using Medications Properly

Most medications have side effects that can affect even healthy aquarium inhabitants. That's why it's important to treat individual fishes in a separate tank. There are also some infectious pathogens, such as *Ichthyopthirius* (see p. 67), whose germs inhabit the whole aquarium. So in many cases the aquarium or the entire water cycle including

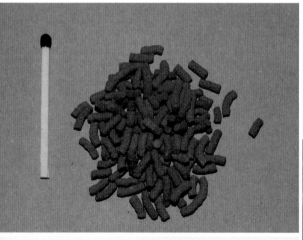

2 **Fishes from soft-water** areas—such as this Vaillant's chocolate gourami—are often more susceptible because their immune systems are not accustomed to elevated concentrations of bacteria encountered in aquariums. They require acidic or relatively bacteria-free water.

1 **Pelletized food** can easily be enriched with vitamins or medications because it is absorbent. Use this method for specific treatments, especially for symptoms of a deficiency.

*Healthy fishes, a dwarf royal
farlowella in this instance, reproduce
even in an aquarium.* ▷

the filter, which then has to keep working, must be treated. Depending on the
medication, this may even harm the
biological filtering effect created by bacteria. In such cases it is important to
determine whether harmful organic
metabolic products such as nitrite and
ammonia are accumulating.

To prevent the accumulation of
harmful organic substances, give the
fishes little or no food for the duration
of the treatment.

As long as the harmful water values
continue to increase, change a significant portion of the water in the aquarium until the harmful effect of the
medications is no longer evident on the
filter medium.

Once the treatment has been com-
pleted according to the directions, use
activated charcoal to filter the leftover
ingredients from the medications out of
the aquarium water.

If separate treatment in an aquarium
or a bucket is necessary for a short
time, continually observe the fishes so
you can cease treatment if you notice
any side effects.

Take water out of the regular tank
and put it into the treatment tank to
keep the fishes from experiencing transfer stress.

Euthanizing Fishes

For vertebrates, including fishes, a quick
severing of the spine with a sharp knife
or scissors right behind the head is
humane. Another possibility that's a
little easier on human sensibilities

involves putting the fish into a bucket
containing a quart/liter of water to
which 5 drops of clove oil (eugenol)
from a pharmacy have been added.
That way the fish is anesthetized. When
the fish lies on its side, add another
10–20 drops until it shows no further
gill movements for quite a while and
ceases responding. Then the fish is
dead. Under no circumstances should
fishes that need to be euthanized be
frozen or flushed down the toilet.

Questions about
Care, Feeding, and Health

? What's the proper way to feed my fishes?

It's best to feed your fishes several times a day, but with only a little food. A good rule of thumb is to feed no more than the fish will eat in 3–5 minutes. Try out several types of food and match the types to the fishes. Look for high-quality ingredients (e.g., spirulina algae and fiber). Put in only as much non-living food into the aquarium as the fishes can eat in a few minutes. To be sure of the quality of both dry and frozen foods, look at the freshness date. Close cans of dry food after feeding and store them in the refrigerator. Don't refreeze frozen food that has thawed and keep thawed food covered in the refrigerator for no longer than a day. If you use an automatic feeder, fill it for only a couple of days since dry food loses quality over time.

? As a preventive measure, should I put a broad-based treatment into the aquarium if I'm not sure whether my fishes are sick and which disease they have?

No. Using broad-based treatments should be considered only if nonspecific symptoms persist, no veterinarians knowledgeable in fish diseases have been able to help, and possible errors in care have been ruled out. If possible, perform the treatment in a separate tank in order to avoid needlessly stressing healthy fishes, plants, and filter bacteria.

? Is it better to use water-conditioning products or perform a partial water change in the aquarium?

Organic substances are introduced into the aquarium water through food and the resulting excrement, and they don't disappear by themselves. Water-conditioning products don't remove the substances from the aquarium but merely bind them in the water and thus make them a little less harmful. But to keep the water free of harmful substances over the long run, these substances must be removed from the water. Water-conditioning products do help in postponing the need for partial water changes, and they are worthwhile in an emergency; however, they are not suitable as replacements for a partial water change. For a regular water change in small aquariums (up to 15 g/54 l), place a filled 2½ gallon (10 l) watering can, a large funnel, a hose 8 feet (2.5 m) long, and an empty 2½ gallon (10 l) bucket near the aquarium. For the weekly water change, use the hose to transfer 2½ gallons (10 l) of water into the bucket through the feeding hatch. Then put the 2½ gallons (10 l) from the watering can into the tank with the funnel, empty the bucket, immediately fill the

watering can with freshwater, and you're done.

How can I keep new fishes from bringing diseases into the aquarium?

Even healthy-appearing fishes can bring disease pathogens into the aquarium, either because they have not yet become ill or because they are immune to the pathogens they are carrying. To make sure that they are not introducing any harmful pathogens, you can set up a quarantine tank. This type of tank consists simply of a small glass aquarium (e.g., 20 × 14 × 12 inches / 50 × 35 × 30 cm), a broken-in filter (which has already been in use for about a month), a heater, and depending on the species of fish, appropriate hiding places (e.g., Java moss, clay pot shards, and tree roots for armored catfishes). You then place your new fishes into this quarantine aquarium. Only after a week or two of

displaying no symptoms of illness should you put them into the regular aquarium. Alternatively, you can of course try to "stake out" fishes from a safe source and watch them for several weeks, for example, in a pet shop near where you live or at a breeder's. If the fishes remain healthy there for several weeks and no new fishes have been introduced in the meantime, you are probably buying healthy fishes. But it's not possible to rule out infection completely.

Can fishes overeat?

Yes, fishes certainly can overeat even when consuming food that's not good for them. In the wild, food is usually scarce. So most fishes are set up to take advantage of every possible opportunity to take in nourishment. In an aquarium, though, there can be an excess of food— only the fishes don't understand this. They keep eating, even when there is too

much, until they can't eat any more. In the long run, overfeeding makes fishes sick, for they gain weight and become sluggish. So feed sparingly.

A while ago my little son dropped the whole can of food into the aquarium. What happens if too much food gets into the water?

The only thing that will help here is a radical water change involving about three-quarters of the tank contents. First siphon out all food immediately with a hose. To play it safe, add some water conditioner from the pet shop to the aquarium after changing the water.

Aquarium and Habitat Profiles

With a realistic aquarium you have a piece of nature in your home. You can experience how fishes, plants, and other aquarium inhabitants create a wonderful society.

Setting Up Realistic Aquariums

Establishing a realistic aquarium requires becoming informed about a specific habitat as you choose and install the future inhabitants. This type of aquarium provides the best possible glimpses of the interplay of nature.

IN THIS CHAPTER I present 10 different tank types with four stocking recommendations each for aquariums of different sizes.

Clarifications on Habitat Aquariums

The stocking and general tank descriptions are oriented, on the one hand, toward the geographic origin of the fishes, and on the other, toward their habitats. Each of these subsections appears on two facing pages: On the first page I describe the type of tank, such as a small South American tank, and give advice about the particular characteristics of the habitat, the aquarium setup, and living conditions. The second page presents suggestions on the stocking for each tank of specific dimensions (length × width × height in inches and cm).

Aquariums That Approximate Habitats

With tanks that are set up according to geographic areas we are not dealing with true biotope tanks but rather with an approximation of natural habitat conditions. Simulating a complete

biotope is not possible in an aquarium, and not even desirable, for you can't take care of predators and prey within the confines of an aquarium. Often the natural habitats of our charges are also not particularly esthetically pleasing, for example, because many waters are cloudy and the substrate is unexciting and often consists of mud. But it is fun to orient ourselves toward a particular type of habitat as we choose fishes and plants. That way you can learn about the natural mixture of species in a habitat. In every subsection I therefore briefly describe the natural habitat type before presenting specific advice about

This dwarf cichlid male is impressive with its natural coloration and behavior, for it has found realistic conditions in the aquarium.

technical devices, setup, planting, and care.

Suggested stocking: The suggested stocking is limited to the species of fishes described in this handbook and provides a glimpse into assembling a compatible mix of aquarium fishes. When the recommendations address the sex of the fishes, the number of

Realistic aquariums provide a habitat that's right for different species of aquarium inhabitants.

males is given first, and then that of the females after the forward slash. An indication of ½, for example, means one male and two females. Not all fish species mentioned for a suggested stocking are always found together into the same body of water. However, they are chosen so that based on their ecology and general geographic origin they could co-exist in the same water and occupy various "ecological niches." Also, you will often find an algae-eating fish species on the list that geographically

doesn't belong in the particular type of habitat. But algae eaters are very useful because they keep algae levels in the aquarium low.

Planting: There can also be inconsistencies in the suggestions for planting because this book favors only a small selection of very easy-to-care-for aquarium plants. Of course, you can avail yourself of species-specific technical literature any time you want to modify these suggestions.

Fish Species That Fit into an Aquarium

After the description of the natural habitat, for example, a large Southeast Asia tank, on the following pages I propose 12 different fish species that correspond to the stocking suggestions.

On the first line I have provided a common English name (when available) for the 12 fish species.

The second line contains the often long, involved Latin name, which consists first of the genus name and, second, the species name. These Latin designations are the international references, and in hobbyist circles are often used more frequently than the English names.

In addition I also provide at this point the maximum size of the relevant fish species.

On the third line you will find information about the water conditions that the particular fish species needs. The water types provided are derived from the carbonate hardness (°dKH) and the acid content (pH level) of the water. Chapter 3 "Water, the Element of Life," starting on p. 36, provides information about the meaning, measurement, and adjustment of water values.

Central American convict cichlid, Cryptoheros nigrofasciatus.

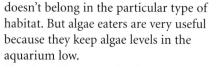

The red back angelfish is a naturally occurring variant of the angelfish. ▶

The seven water types are:
Water Type 1: pH 4.5–6.5; °dKH 0–3
Water Type 2: pH 5.5–6.8; °dKH 3–8
Water Type 3: pH 6.8–7.5; °dKH 3–8
Water Type 4: pH 6.8–7.5; °dKH 8–16
Water Type 5: pH 7.2–8.5; °dKH >12
Water Type 6: pH 8.0–9.5; °dKH 0–3
Water Type 7: pH 8.0–9.5; °dKH >12, enriched with two to three additional teaspoons of sea salt per $2\frac{1}{2}$ gallons/ 10 liters of water (see "The Brackish-Water Tank," p. 112).

Specifying the water types involves empirical values that provide good living conditions.

The fourth line indicates a guideline for the minimum tank size appropriate for adult fishes of the given species. **Note:** Fishes that are not fully grown generally require less space. However, when you purchase young fishes you have to consider their eventual size. Fishes that don't reach their expected size in an aquarium generally are not getting the right care. This is true even though it is continually reported in the aquarium trade that the final size adjusts to the tank. This is not true and results only from improper living conditions.

Frogs, Shrimps, Crabs, and Snails

In a brief additional chapter starting on p. 116 you will learn about taking care of African dwarf clawed frogs, shrimps, crabs, prawns, and snails. They are kept in aquariums with increasing frequency. No wonder, for these often colorful and amusing creatures fascinate many aquarists. In some ways these species are ideal because they can be kept with fishes in community aquariums as long as you observe a few rules.

A Small South American Tank

When you select this type of habitat, you simulate a peaceful section of a calm, clear rain forest stream. Here you can combine colorful schooling fishes with earthy Armored Catfishes.

MANY FAVORITE aquarium fishes come from South America. A large number of them come from brooks and small rivers in the jungle or savanna, which don't contain much food and have slightly to very acidic water. These flowing waters have crystal-clear water, at least during the dry season, in which rich underwater plant growth can go wild. Although the water is clear, it is often a dark tea color (black water). The shimmering, luminous colors of many jungle stream inhabitants, such as the neon and cardinal tetras, are shown to good advantage in the half-light of jungle streams.

Tank Type: Heavily Planted Tropical Stream

The charm of a fairly small South American tank lies in the possibility of combining colorful schooling fishes (usually from the charactin or tetra family) with cute corydoras and earthy armored catfishes in a nicely planted tank. In slightly larger tanks another few pairs of dwarf cichlids can be added.

General note on care: Fine gravel (sandy in some places for corydoras), a fairly dark substrate with one or more small tree roots and thick edge planting, but also some open-swimming room. An inside cartridge filter or outside canister filter, a heater, two fluorescent tubes the same length as the tank, one oxygen releaser, $2\frac{1}{2}$ inches (6 cm) of fine gravel, to which as been added controlled-release fertilizer. In feeding with a variety of dry and frozen food, make sure the corydoras and armored

INFO

Tetras Characins (Tetras)

The approximately 1500 species of characins, also known as tetras (Characiformes) are distributed among various fish families, of which most occur in South America and Africa. Among others, characins include such favorite aquarium families as the freshwater hatchetfishes, African tetras, hemiodus, South American tetras, piranhas and their relatives, and the Pink-tailed chalceus. Most characins are predominantly schooling fishes. The famous neon and cardinal tetras fishes also are characins. Representatives of this large group make up the lion's share of aquarium fishes sold on the market.

Beautiful to look at: Newly set up and stocked small South American tank.

catfishes aren't short-changed. The lively schooling fishes are often quicker in snapping up the food and take the best morsels away from the catfishes. It thus makes sense to feed these fishes once again with food tablets, for example, after shutting off the light.
Planting: One to three roots, black sword plant, dwarf sword plant, Java moss, creeping red ludwigia, Brazilian pennywort.

Suggested stocking No. 1 (24 × 12 × 14 in. / 60 × 30 × 35 cm):

▶ 12 characins that remain small (neons, glowlight tetras) or guppies
▶ 5 otocinclus catfishes
▶ 5 corydoras

Suggested stocking No. 2 (24 × 12 × 14 in. / 60 × 30 × 35 cm):

▶ 1 pair of dwarf cichlids or 6 rosy tetras

▶ 5 otocinclus catfishes
▶ 6 Anduzi's nannostomus, or other pencilfish, or freshwater hatchetfishes

Suggested stocking No. 3 (40 × 16 × 16 in. / 100 × 40 × 40 cm):

▶ 1 pair of bristlenosed catfishes
▶ 25 characins that remain small (neons, glowlight tetras) or guppies
▶ 6 freshwater hatchetfishes
▶ 6 rosy tetras
▶ 6 corydoras

Suggested stocking No. 4 (40 × 16 × 16 in. / 100 × 40 × 40 cm):

▶ 10 otocinclus catfishes
▶ 2 pairs of dwarf cichlids
▶ 12 Anduzi's nannostomus or other pencilfish and 12 freshwater hatchetfishes

A black-water stream with extreme water values (water type 1).

Fish Profiles

The suggested stockings with these fishes are listed on p. 77.

❶ Neon Tetra
Paracheirodon innesi; 1½ inches (4 cm)
Water type: 1–5; 68–75°F (20–24°C)
Minimum tank size: 13 gallons (50 l)

❷ Cardinal Tetra
Paracheirodon axelrodi; 1½ inches (4 cm)
Water type: 2–5; 77–82°F (25–28°C)
Minimum tank size: 13 gallons (50 l)

❸ Black Neon Tetra
Hyphessobrycon herbertaxelrodi; 1½ inches (4 cm)
Water type: 2–4; 75–82°F (24–28°C)
Minimum tank size: 13 gallons (50 l)

❹ Rosy Tetra
Hyphessobrycon rosaceus; 1¾ inches (4.5 cm)
Water type: 2–5; 73–80°F (23–27°C)
Minimum tank size: 13 gallons (50 l)

❺ Marbled Hatchetfish
Carnegiella strigata; 1½ inches (4 cm)
Water type: 1–4; 79–86°F (26–30°C)
Minimum tank size: 14 gallons (50 l)

❻ Guppy
Poecilia reticulata; 2½ inches (6 cm)
Water type: 2–5; 75–86°F (24–30°C)
Minimum tank size: 14 gallons (50 l)

❼ Three-lined Cory
Corydoras trilineatus; 2½ inches (6 cm)
Water type: 2–5; 77–82°F (25–28°C)
Minimum tank size: 14 gallons (50 l)

❽ Panda Cory
Corydoras panda; 2 inches (5 cm)
Water type: 2–6; 73–79°F (23–26°C)
Minimum tank size: 14 gallons (50 l)

❾ *Otocinculus* sp. 1½ inches (4 cm)
Water type: 2–6; 71–80°F (22–27°C)
Minimum tank size: 14 gallons (50 l)

❿ Bristlenosed Catfish
Ancistrus sp.; 5½ inches (14 cm)
Water type: 2–6; 75–83°F (24–29°C)
Minimum tank size: 28 gallons (100 l)

⓫ Ram Cichlid
Microgeophagus ramirezi; 2 inches (5 cm)
Water type: 1–3; 79–86°F (26–30°C)
Minimum tank size: 14 gallons (50 l)

⓬ Yellow Dwarf Cichlid
Apistogramma borellii; 2¾ inches (7 cm)
Water type: 2–4; 71–75°F (22–24°C)
Minimum tank size: 14 gallons (50 l)

Popular Species for
Small South American Tanks

A Large South American Tank

The charm of this aquarium lies in the fact that here you can create a dimly lit jungle ambience. The fishes include a combination of fairly large catfishes, colorful cichlids, and medium-sized characins.

THE FAIRLY LARGE jungle rivers in South America are home to many aquarium fishes. One characteristic of these waters important to aquarium hobbyists is the many jungle trees and their decomposed remains lying in the water, which provide a home and shelter for many amusing catfishes and cichlids. On the one hand, the pieces of wood with branches and natural caves provide shelter especially for catfishes, many of which take care of their fry, and on the other hand, the rotting wood serves as food for the tiniest creatures, which in turn provide food for the fishes. Some armored catfishes even grate off the difficult-to-digest wood as fiber for use in digestion, and they would die if they didn't have a supply of wood in the aquarium.

Tank Type: River or Fairly Large Brook with Deadwood

If you choose carefully, you can easily place fairly large catfishes and sumptuous cichlids with characins that love to swim. The planting can be limited to a few species that are not demanding in terms of light. It's best to arrange lots of large tree roots in the tank so that they look like naturally waterlogged deadwood or submerged roots of living trees along the bank.

General note on care: High-performance outside canister filter, a heater, two fluorescent tubes the length of the tank, $2\frac{1}{2}$ inches (6 cm) of fine gravel or coarse sand, controlled-release fertilizer in numerous locations (for the

INFO

Catfishes

With more than 2000 species, the catfishes are a very rich order of fishes with lots of families on all continents. The South American armored catfish (callichthyidae) and the armored sucker-mouthed catfish are of particular importance to aquarium hobbyists. The most popular representative of the former are catfishes of the genus *Corydoras*. The Mochokidae are a particularly popular catfish from Africa. Catfishes are often regarded as "garbage disposals" in the aquarium, which nearly automatically leads to errors in providing care. The various armored sucker-mouthed catfish species often have difficult food requirements.

A lushly planted large South American tank in which bleeding heart tetra dominate.

Echinodorus plants). The lighting can consist of one or two fluorescent tubes per tank length, or depending on the length of the tank, one to three metal halide spotlights (70 W).

Planting: Five to ten large roots with slender "branches," sword plants (*Echinodorus*), Java moss, and Brazilian pennywort.

Suggested stocking No. 1 (40 × 20 × 24 in. / 100 × 50 × 60 cm)

▸ 6 angelfishes
▸ 15 rummy-nose tetras
▸ 1 pair blue bristlenosed catfishes or similar *Ancistrus* species
▸ 6 flagtail corydoras

Suggested stocking No. 2 (40 × 20 × 24 in. / 100 × 50 × 60 cm)

▸ 1/2 lyretail checkerboard cichlids or other South American dwarf cichlids (*Apistogramma, Laetacara*)

▸ 10 diamond tetras, bleeding heart tetras, or emperor tetras
▸ 10 *otocinclus* sp. *hoppei*

Suggested stocking No. 3 (60 × 20 × 24 in. / 150 × 50 × 60 cm)

▸ 8 altum angelfishes or discus fishes
▸ 10 silver hatchetfishes
▸ 1 pair dwarf royal farlowellas
▸ 6 flagtail corydoras
▸ 10 *otocinclus* sp. *hoppei*

Suggested stocking No. 4 (60 × 20 × 24 in. / 150 × 50 × 60 cm)

▸ 1 pair *Mesonauta insignis*
▸ 1 pair blue bristlenosed catfishes
▸ 10 slender hemiodus
▸ 10 diamond tetras or bleeding heart tetras
▸ 10 corydoras

Popular Species for
Large South American Tanks

Fish Profiles

The suggested stockings with these fish species are found on p. 81.

❶ Rummy-nose tetra
Hemigrammus bleheri; 1¾ in (4.5 cm)
Water type: 1–3; 71–79°F (22–26°C)
Minimum tank size: 40 gallons (150 l)

❷ Diamond Tetra
Moenkhausia pittieri; 2½ in (6 cm)
Water type: 2–4; 75–82°F (24–28°C)
Minimum tank size: 66 gallons (250 l)

❸ Bleeding Heart Tetra
Hyphessobrycon erythrostigma; 3 in (8 cm)
Water type: 2–4; 75–82°F (24–28°C)
Minimum tank size: 66 gallons (250 l)

❹ Silver Hatchetfish
Thoracocharax secures; 3½ in (9 cm)
Water type: 2–4; 77–86°F (25–30°C)
Minimum tank size: 93 gallons (350 l)

❺ Slender Hemiodus
Hemiodopsis gracilis; 7 in (18 cm)
Water type: 2–4; 75–82°F (24–28°C)
Minimum tank size: 185 gallons (700 l)

❻ Flagtail Corydoras
Corydoras robinae; 2¾ in (7 cm)
Water type: 2–4; 75–82°F (24–28°C)
Minimum tank size: 28 gallons (100 l)

❼ Flagtail Armored or Hoplo Catfish
Dianema urostriata; 4 in (10 cm)
Water type: 2–5; 77–82°F (25–28°C)
Minimum tank size: 69 gallons (250 l)

❽ Festivum or Flag Cichlid
Mesonauta insignis; 8 in (20 cm)
Water type: 2–5; 75–86°F (24–30°C)
Minimum tank size: 83 gallons (300 l)

▲

Fallen branches at the edge of the water offer shelter to many fishes.

❾ Altum Angelfish
Pterophyllym altum; 6–13 in (15–33 cm) tall
Water type: 1–2; 80–86°F (27–30°C)
Minimum tank size: 138 gallons (500 l); tank height at least 27½ in (70 cm)

❿ Angelfish
Pterophyllum scalare; 6–10 in (15 to 26 cm) tall
Water type: 2–4; 77–84°F (25–29°C)
Minimum tank size: 69 gallons (250 l); tank height at least 24 in (60 cm)

⓫ Discus Fish
Symphysodon aequifasciata; 7 in (18 cm)
Water type: 2; 79–86°F (26–30°C)
Minimum tank size: 69 gallons (250 l)

⓬ Lyretail Checkerboard Cichlid
Dicrossus filamentosus; 3½ in (9 cm)
Water type: 1–2; 80–86°F (27–30°C)
Minimum tank size: 41 gallons (150 l)

A West African Tank

Fishes that are at home in the brooks and rivers of West Africa are some of the most colorful of all aquarium fishes. When you set up this type of West African tank, you introduce pure jungle flair into your home.

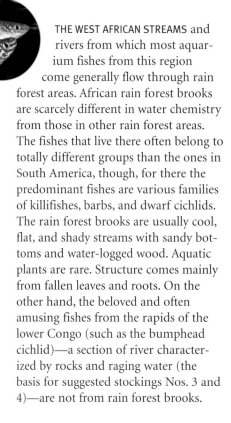

THE WEST AFRICAN STREAMS and rivers from which most aquarium fishes from this region come generally flow through rain forest areas. African rain forest brooks are scarcely different in water chemistry from those in other rain forest areas. The fishes that live there often belong to totally different groups than the ones in South America, though, for there the predominant fishes are various families of killifishes, barbs, and dwarf cichlids. The rain forest brooks are usually cool, flat, and shady streams with sandy bottoms and water-logged wood. Aquatic plants are rare. Structure comes mainly from fallen leaves and roots. On the other hand, the beloved and often amusing fishes from the rapids of the lower Congo (such as the bumphead cichlid)—a section of river characterized by rocks and raging water (the basis for suggested stockings Nos. 3 and 4)—are not from rain forest brooks.

Various Tank Types

Suggested stocking No. 1 is based on a tiny rain forest brook in which the colorful killifishes are nearly the only inhabitants. These fishes are best kept by themselves, and yet they are so colorful and lively that it is still worthwhile to have a small tank kept dark for these gems of the jungle. It's often difficult to keep killifishes in a mixed-species tank because they should be kept cooler. A killifish tank has the character of a dusky jungle brook. The other suggested stockings correspond in type to that for the small or large South American tank. They are dominated by roots and plants that can be well illuminated and are more appropriate to the type of "sunny, clear-water brook" (see pp. 76 and 80).

INFO

Killifishes

Killifishes is the common name applied to the nearly worldwide egg-laying tooth carps (*Cyprinodontiformes*) of various families. In this book they are represented by the African *Aphyosemion* and the Tanganyikan killifishes. The *Aphyosemion* species include some of the most colorful freshwater fishes of all. Many *Aphyosemion* reproduce in a special way. They are equipped to produce resting eggs, which they can deposit on the moist bottom. If the water dries up, the parents die, but the buried eggs survive, and when the first rain comes, the next generation hatches from the eggs.

Congo tetra in a tank nicely arranged with giant Anubias.

General notes on care: Life support equipment and decor for these tanks, as for the small South American tank (see p. 76), and the large South American tank (see p. 80) depend on the size of the tank. With suggested stocking No. 1, set up the tank so that the *Aphyosemion* find quiet, dark-water areas and the lampeyes, on the other hand, can have a gentle current.

Planting: Java fern, Java moss, floating broadleaf water sprite.

Suggested stocking No. 1 (24 × 12 × 14 in. / 60 × 30 × 35 cm)

▶ 4/6 *Aphyosemion*
▶ 6 large-finned lampeye

Suggested stocking No. 2 (40 × 16 × 16 in. / 100 × 40 × 40 cm)

▶ 1 pair common nib or other *Pelvicachromis* species
▶ 6 back-swimming Congo catfishes

▶ 12 long-finned lampeyes
▶ 8 *Otocinclus hoppei*

Suggested stocking No. 3 (40 × 16 × 16 in. / 100 × 40 × 40 cm)

▶ 1 pair bumphead cichlids
▶ 1 pair common kribs
▶ 1 pair bristlenosed catfishes
▶ 8 blue Congo tetras or pink-tailed chalceus

Suggested stocking No. 4 (60 × 20 × 20 in. / 150 × 50 × 50 cm)

▶ 1 pair bumphead cichlids
▶ 1 pair common kribs
▶ 1 pair bristlenosed catfishes
▶ 20 African long-finned tetras, Congo tetras, or African red-eye characins
▶ 12 upside-down catfishes

Kribensis and other fishes live in
clear jungle brooks.

Fish Profiles

The suggested stockings with these
fishes are found on p. 85.

❶ African Red-eye Characin
Arnoldicthys spilopterus; 3 in (8 cm)
Water type: 2–4; 75–82°F (24–28°C)
Minimum tank size: 69 gallons (250 l)

❷ African Longfin Tetra
Brycinus longipinnis; 5 in (13 cm)
Water type: 2–5; 75–84°F (24–29°C)
Minimum tank size: 110 gallons (400 l)

❸ Congo Tetra
Phenacogrammus interruptus; $3\frac{1}{2}$ in
(9 cm)
Water type: 2–4; 73–81°F (23–27°C)
Minimum tank size: 83 gallons (300 l)

❹ Steel-blue Lyretail Killifish
Fundulopanchax gardneri; $2\frac{3}{4}$ in (7 cm)
Water type: 2–4; 73–80°F (23–27°C)
Minimum tank size: 14 gallons (50 l)

❺ Red-lined Killifish
Aphyosemion striatum; 2 in (5 cm)
Water type: 2–5; 70–73°F (21–23°C)
Minimum tank size: 14 gallons (50 l)

❻ Large-finned Lampeye
Procatopus nototaenia; 2 in (5 cm)
Water type: 2–5; 72–77°F (22–25°C)
Minimum tank size: 41 gallons (150 l)

❼ Upside-down Catfish
Synodontis nigriventris; $3\frac{1}{4}$ in (8 cm)
Water type: 2–5; 75–82°F (24–28°C)
Minimum tank size: 41 gallons (150 l)

❽ Purple Krib
Pelvicachromis taeniatus; $3\frac{1}{4}$ in (8 cm)
Water type: 2–4; 75–80°F (24–27°C)
Minimum tank size: 14 gallons (50 l)

❾ Common Krib
Pelvicachromis pulcher; 4 in (10 cm)
Water type: 2–5; 77–82° (25–28°C)
Minimum tank size: 28 gallons (100 l)

❿ Congo Dwarf Mouthbrooder
Pseudocrenilabrus nicholsi; $3\frac{1}{4}$ in (8 cm)
Water type: 2–5; 75–80°F (24–27°C)
Minimum tank size: 28 gallons (100 l)

⓫ Dwarf Jewel Fish
Anomalochromis thomasi; $3\frac{1}{4}$ in (8 cm)
Water type: 2–4; 75–82°F (24–28°C)
Minimum tank size: 28 gallons (100 l)

⓬ Bumphead or Buffalohead Cichlid
Steatocranus casuarius; $5\frac{1}{2}$ in (14 cm)
Water type: 3–6; 75–82°F (24–28°C)
Minimum tank size: 41 gallons (150 l)

Popular Species for
West African Tanks

A Small Southeast Asian Tank

What should it be? A small central mountain stream or a weedy swamp? The fishes and plants described here come from both habitats. The choice is entirely up to you.

THE TYPICAL HABITATS of small Asian fish species are either small jungle brooks or thickly planted swamps. While forest streams containing fishes from the suggested stocking described here often have sandy bottoms with gravel and resemble low-altitude mountain streams, a great many small fishes live in the heavily planted swamp waters with stagnant or slightly moving water. Even the beloved fighting fishes come from swampy waters. They also live in flooded rice fields.

Various Tank Types

The tank type for suggested stocking No. 1 is a simulation of a small, low-altitude mountain stream: A bottom of fine, not necessarily dark, gravel, pebbles, and bright lighting. The current in many tanks can be strengthened somewhat with a submerged powerhead. Crypts are the main plants. The tank types for the other suggested stockings correspond to the weedy swamp habitat. Heavy plant growth is encouraged through good lighting and a sandy, gravelly substrate rich in nutrients.

Small, slender roots provide hiding places for loaches, and floating plants allow bubble-nesting labyrinth fishes to feel at home. The current is weak. **General notes on care:** In the "weed tanks" (suggested stocking Nos. 2–4), avoid significant movement in the water by reducing the filter outlet if necessary. But with tank type 1, use an inside motor filter to provide good current

INFO

Labyrinth Fishes

The Labyrinth fishes include more than 100 species that are distributed in Africa and Asia. Nearly all species are distinguished by an additional breathing organ (a "labyrinth"), with which they can breathe atmospheric air. Thus they can also survive in swampy water with little oxygen. Most of them are territorial, at least prior to spawning and while caring for their fry. Then the males of many species, such as the thick-lip gouramis, the croaking gouramis, and the fighting fishes mentioned here, build a foam nest out of saliva-coated air bubbles in a quiet location on the surface of the water.

Lively barbs, rasboras, and labyrinth fishes romp in a small Southeast Asian tank.

(turn it off for feeding); lighting with two fluorescent bulbs. Lots of variety in feeding, with fine dry and frozen food (e.g., Cyclops). Add *Macrotocinclus hoppei* in case of algae problems.
Planting: Corkscrew *Vallisneria*, Wendtii crypts, *Cryptocoryne beckettii*, Java fern, Java moss, water hyssop, creeping red ludwigia, floating water sprite, and Crystalwort.

Suggested stocking No. 1 (24 × 12 × 14 in. / 60 × 30 × 35 cm)
▶ 1/3 white-cheek gobies
▶ 8 checkered barbs
▶ 10 zebra fishes

Suggested stocking No. 2 (24 × 12 × 14 in. / 60 × 30 × 35 cm)
▶ 2/2 pygmy croaking gouramis
▶ 15 green-eye rasboras
▶ 6 kuhlii loaches

Suggested stocking No. 3 (24 × 12 × 14 in. / 60 × 30 × 35 cm)
▶ 1/1 siamese fighting fishes
▶ 8 harlequin rasboras
▶ 6 dwarf loaches

Suggested stocking No. 4 (32 × 12 × 16 in. / 80 × 35 × 40 cm)
▶ 1/1 dwarf gouramis
▶ 15 harlequin rasboras
▶ 12 green-eye rasboras
▶ 8 dwarf loaches

Popular Species for Small
Southeast Asian Tanks

Fish Profiles

The suggested stockings with these fishes are on page 89.

❶ **Harlequin or Red Rasbora**
Trigonostigma heteromorpha; 1¾ inches (4.5 cm)
Water type: 2–5; 73–82°F (23–28°C)
Minimum tank size: 14 gallons (50 l)

❷ **Green-eye Rasbora**
Rasbora dorsiocellata; 2½ inches (6 cm)
Water type: 2–5, 73–82°F (23–28°C)
Minimum tank size: 14 gallons (50 l)

❸ **White Cloud**
Tanichthys albonubes; 1½ inches (4 cm)
Water type: 2–6; 64–72°F / 18–22°C
Minimum tank size: 14 gallons (50 l)

❹ **Zebra Fish**
Danio rerio; 2 inches (5 cm)
Water type: 2–6; 73–80°F / 23–27°C
Minimum tank size: 14 gallons (50 l)

❺ **Checkered Barb**
Puntius oligolepis; 2 inches (5 cm)
Water type: 2–6; 73–80°F / 23–27°C
Minimum tank size: 14 gallons (50 l)

❻ **Kuhlii Loach**
Pangio kuhlii; 3 inches (8 cm)
Water type: 2–6; 79–86°F / 24–30°
Minimum tank size: 14 gallons (50 l)

❼ **Dwarf Loach**
Yasuhikotakia sidthimunki; 2½ inches (6 cm)
Water type: 2–6; 79–84°F / 26–29°C
Minimum tank size: 14 gallons (50 l)

❽ **Dwarf Gourami**
Colisa lalia; 2½ inches (6 cm)

▲

Stony brooks are the typical habitat for many loaches and rasboras.

Water type: 2–6; 75–82°F / 24–28°C
Minimum tank size: 14 gallons (50 l)

❾ **Honey Gourami**
Colisa chuna; 2 inches (5 cm)
Water type: 2–6; 72–82°F / 22–28°C
Minimum tank size: 14 gallons (50 l)

❿ **Siamese Fighting Fish**
Betta splendens; 2½ inches (6 cm)
Water type: 2–6; 75–82°F / 24–28°C
Minimum tank size: 14 gallons (50 l)

⓫ **Pygmy Croaking Gourami**
Trichopsis pumila; 1½ inches (4 cm)
Water type: 2–6; 73–80°F / 23–27°C
Minimum tank size: 14 gallons (50 l)

⓬ **White-checked Goby**
Rhinogobius cf. wui; 2 inches (5 cm)
Water type: 4–6; 64–75°F / 18–24°C
Minimum tank size: 14 gallons (50 l)

A Large Southeast Asian Tank

In this aquarium there should be running water with "forests" composed of crypts, open bottom areas, and weedy corners. This is the kind of place where such fishes as barbs, rasboras, and spiny eels are comfortable.

THE HABITATS of many fairly large Asian aquarium fishes can be rather large brooks thickly grown with crypts, small rivers with clear water, or larger rivers that flow through broad alluvial plains that lead through rain forest or open savanna landscapes. As in South America and Africa there is a group of favorite schooling fishes (mainly barbs and rasboras) near the bottom of the open water, whereas catfishes, loaches, and spiny eels find hiding places in the lush tangles of plant structures or mangled roots. Labyrinth fishes and blue panchax prefer the weedy shore areas with practically no current.

Tank Type

Depending on the size of the tank, it is possible to simulate the nature of the fairly large Asian flowing waters described above. The possibility of combining crypt forests with open bottoms and weedy corners in the aquarium for still-water fishes presents an opportunity to display the unique character of the very lively barbs and rasboras in a well-lighted tank. Spiny eels and barbs need some soft substrate for digging.

Siamese algae eaters like to scrape algae from wood roots that lie in the current. General notes on care: See "A Large South American Tank," p. 80.

In planting you needn't scrimp on *Cryptocoryne beckettii.* You can use a substrate of fine gravel with sand in some places. Thorough filtering with a large-volume exterior canister filter is

INFO

Carps and Other Allies

There are about 2000 species of carp-like fishes (Cyprinidae) native to North America, Eurasia, and Africa. The various carp groups are quite distinct from one another in appearance alone. Barbs and rasboras belong among the fairly "normal type" of fishes; the usually bottom-dwelling loaches such as *Pangio kuhlii*, may be elongated like snakes. Most relatives of the carp don't take care of their fry but rather scatter their eggs in the water, on aquatic plants, or over gravel. Like catfishes, they often have sensitive whiskers on their snouts.

The wonderful silver sharks display their typical beauty only in very large aquariums.

best. Two fluorescent bulbs the same length as the tank are adequate for crypts (three are better for larger tanks). Feeding with all common types of food; make sure that the spiny eels get enough food or else feed them frozen food after turning off the lighting.

Planting: Wendtii crypts, Beckett's crypts, various types of large crypts (depending on the tank size), Java fern, Java moss, water hyssop, Indian swamp-weed.

Suggested stocking No. 1 (48 × 20 × 20 in. / 120 × 50 × 50 cm)

▸ 1/3 three-spot gouramis
▸ 12 black ruby barbs
▸ 5 siamese flying foxes
▸ 3 spot-finned spiny eels

Suggested stocking No. 2 (48 × 20 × 20 in. / 120 × 50 × 50 cm)

▸ 12 odessa barbs
▸ 20 zebra fishes
▸ 5 siamese flying foxes
▸ 6 spot-finned spiny eels

Suggested stocking No. 3 (48 × 20 × 20 in. / 120 × 50 × 50 cm)

▸ 1/1 pearl gouramis
▸ 5 siamese flying foxes
▸ 10 red-lined torpedo barbs
▸ 6 spot-finned spiny eels

Suggested stocking No. 4 (100 × 24 × 24 in. / 250 × 60 × 60 cm)

▸ 8 clown loaches
▸ 1 red-tailed black shark
▸ 12 bala or silver sharks
▸ 15 giant danios

Leaves and deadwood from the surrounding rain forest determine the structure of the habitat.

Fish Profiles

The suggested stockings with these fish species appear on page 93.

❶ Giant Danio
Devario aequipinnatus; 4 in (10 cm)
Water type: 2–6; 75–80° F (24–27°C)
Minimum tank size: 69 gallons (250 l)

❷ Red-lined Torpedo Barb
Puntius denisonii; $6\frac{1}{4}$ in (16 cm)
Water type: 3–5; 73–80°F (23–27°C)
Minimum tank size: 110 gallons (400 l)
(also see photo, front cover flap)

❸ Siamese Flying Fox
Crossocheilus oblongus; 6 in (15 cm)
Water type: 2–5; 75–82°F (24–28°C)
Minimum tank size: 83 gallons (300 l)

❹ Red-tailed Black Shark
Epalzeorhynchus bicolor; 6 in (15 cm)
Water type: 2–6; 73–82°F (23–28°C)
Minimum tank size: 83 gallons (300 l)

❺ Odessa Barb
Puntius sp. 'Odessa'; $2\frac{3}{4}$ in (7 cm)
Water type: 2–6; 72–77°F (22–25°C)
Minimum tank size: 41 gallons (150 l)

❻ Clown Loach
Chromobotia macracantha; 10 in
(25 cm)
Water type: 1–5; 77–86°F (25–30°C)
Minimum tank size: 206 gallons (750 l)

❼ Bala or Silver Shark
Balantiocheilos melanopterus; $13\frac{3}{4}$ in
(35 cm)
Water type: 2–5; 75–82°F (24–28°C)
Minimum tank size: 250 gallons (900 l)

❽ Black Ruby Barb
Puntius nigrofasciatus; $2\frac{3}{4}$ in (7 cm)
Water type: 2–5; 71–75°F (21–24°C)
Minimum tank size: 41 gallons (150 l)

❾ Striped Panchax
Aplocheilus lineatus; $4\frac{3}{4}$ in (12 cm)
Water type: 2–6; 75–83°F (24–29°C)
Minimum tank size: 28 gallons (100 l)

❿ Three-spot Gourami
Trichogaster trichopterus; $4\frac{3}{4}$ in (12 cm)
Water type: 2–6; 72–80°F (22–27°C)
Minimum tank size: 41 gallons (150 l)

⓫ Pearl Gourami
Trichogaster leerii; $4\frac{3}{4}$ in (12 cm)
Water type: 2–4; 77–84°F (22–27°C)
Minimum tank size: 41 gallons (150 l)

⓬ Spot-finned Spiny Eel
Macrognathus siamensis; 12 in (30 cm)
Water type: 2–5; 73–80°F (23–27°C)
Minimum tank size: 83 gallons (300 l)

Popular Species for
Large Southeast Asian Tanks

An Australasian Tank

This aquarium will give you a breath of Australia and New Guinea in your home: Flooded with sunshine, crystal-clear, gently moving water, lots of plants, and plenty of free-swimming room for the colorful fishes.

THERE ARE MANY PREY FISHES that are found only in Australia and New Guinea, and the aquatic world in that region is characterized by many special features. Brooks, rivers, swamps, and lakes are not fundamentally different in character from those of other regions but rather in the animals and plants that live in them. Rainbowfishes live only in this region; they inhabit mainly clear running water or lakes. Their brilliant colors, which are displayed mainly by adult males, are seen to best advantage in the morning sun at the edge of aquatic plant thickets flooded with sunlight. In contrast to West African or South American waters, Australian bodies of water often contain more nutrients and are less acidic. Thus most Australian fishes can often be kept in tap water and are not very demanding with respect to the chemical values of the water.

Tank Type: Rainbowfish Tank

The type of tank is tailored to the requirements of Rainbowfishes and their relatives. Most species like tanks flooded with sunlight and crystal-clear water and rich plant growth, and especially lots of room for open swimming. A gentle current with plants swaying in the water completes the picture, along with some fine tree roots. These tanks reveal their greatest splendor when they receive direct morning sunlight. Then the courting male rainbowfishes

INFO

Old World Silversides

Rainbowfishes, halfbeaks, and blue-eyes are part of this fish group. Most other members live in the ocean. That's why the freshwater species prefer "salty" water, that is, hard, alkaline water, and should not be kept in acidic, soft water (and yet there are exceptions). None of the species brood their young but rather lay eggs attached to various objects by threads. Halfbeaks, on the other hand, are mostly live-bearing. Rainbowfishes and blue-eyes are particularly social fishes.

This tank contains all the requirements for the development of young rainbowfishes.

positively glow. The substrate should be fine gravel, and there should be a few small, cylindrical hiding places for sedate gobies, which are the only fishes that need a little open bottom (suggested tank No. 1).

General notes on care: Good illumination with two to four fluorescent bulbs (for small and large tanks, respectively) provides for intensive plant growth. Otherwise like the small South American tank, p. 76.

Planting: Corkscrew *Vallisneria*, dwarf *Sagittaria*, Wendtii crypts, *Cryptocoryne beckettii*, Java fern, Java moss, *Najas conferta*.

Suggested stocking No. 1 (24 × 12 × 14 in. / 50 × 30 × 35 cm)

- ▶ 1/2 peacock or desert gobies
- ▶ 10 spotted blue-eyes
- ▶ 6 *Otocinclus* sp.

Suggested Stocking No. 2 (32 × 14 × 16 in. / 80 × 35 × 40 cm)

- ▶ 3/5 threadfin rainbowfishes
- ▶ 8 *Otocinclus* sp.

Suggested stocking No. 3 (40 × 16 × 16 in. / 100 × 40 × 40 cm)

- ▶ 8 celebes rainbowfishes or 8 forktail blue-eyes
- ▶ 8 neon rainbowfishes or any other *Melanotaenia* that will remain small
- ▶ 1/1 bristlenosed catfishes

Suggested stocking No. 4 (63 × 24 × 24 in. / 160 × 60 × 60 cm)

- ▶ 10 fairly large *Melanotaenia* sp.
- ▶ 10 *Chilatherina* sp.
- ▶ 10 *Glossolepis* sp.
- ▶ 6 siamese flying foxes

Popular Species for
Australasian Tanks

Fish Profiles

The suggested stockings with these fishes can be found on page 97.

❶ Tami River Rainbowfish
Glossolepis pseudoincisus; 3½ inches (9 cm)
Water type: 4–6; 73–79°F (23–26°C)
Minimum tank size: 41 gallons (150 l)

❷ Bleher's Rainbowfish
Chilatherina bleheri; 5½ inches (14 cm)
Water type: 4–6; 77–82°F (25–28°C)
Minimum tank size: 96 gallons (350 l)

❸ Neon Rainbowfish
Melanotaenia praecox; 2½ inches (6 cm)
Water type: 2–5; 73–80°F (23–27°C)
Minimum tank size: 28 gallons (100 l)

❹ Boesman's Rainbowfish
Melanotaenia boesemani; 5½ inches (14 cm)
Water type: 4–6; 77–82°F (25–28°C)
Minimum tank size: 83 gallons (300 l)

❺ Banded Rainbowfish
Melanotaenia trifasciata; 6 inches (15 cm)
Water type: 4–6; 75–82°F (24–28°C)
Minimum tank size: 165 gallons (600 l)

❻ Threadfin Rainbowfish
Iriatherina werneri; 2 inches (5 cm)
Water type: 2–5; 77–86°F (25–30°C)
Minimum tank size: 28 gallons (100 l)

❼ Forktail Blue-eye
Popondichthys furcatus; 2½ inches (6 cm)
Water type: 3–5; 75–80°F (24–27°C)
Minimum tank size: 14 gallons (50 l)

❽ Spotted Blue-eye
Pseudomugil gertrudae; 1½ inches (4 cm)

A beautiful rainbowfish habitat with lots of aquatic plants in Australia.

Water type: 2–5; 77–82°F (24–27°C)
Minimum tank size: 14 gallons (50 l)

❾ Celebes Rainbowfish
Marosatherina ladigesi; 2¾ inches (7 cm)
Water type: 4–6; 77–82°F (25–28°C)
Minimum tank size: 41 gallons (150 l)

❿ Celebes Halfbeak
Nomorhamphus liemi; 3½ inches (9 cm)
Water type: 3–5; 68–75°F (20–24°C)
Minimum tank size: 41 gallons (150 l)

⓫ Peacock Goby
Tateurndina ocellicauda; 2 inches (5 cm)
Water type: 2–5; 79–84°F (26–29°C)
Minimum tank size: 14 gallons (50 l)

⓬ Desert Goby
Chlamydogobius eremius; 2½ inches (6 cm)
Water type: 4–6; 54–79°F (12–26°C)
Minimum tank size: 14 gallons (50 l)

A Central American Tank

Do you like large aquariums? If you do, I recommend a Central American tank with a gentle current, crystal-clear water, and protruding roots that offer a retreat for the fairly gentle fish species.

CENTRAL AMERICAN STREAMS and rivers have greenish clear or milky water because of their usually high lime content. Whether they flow through karstic and sunny habitats or through jungles, their turquoise-colored water over a stony bottom gives Central American bodies of water a special note. Most of these waters have a fairly fast current and abundant algae growth, which makes up the nutritional basis for the fishes in this region, the live-bearing tooth carps. These fishes dart about in groups, usually feeding on the growth, and the males in their ongoing courtship rituals are impressive with their gaudy colors and frantic movements. Amazingly colorful cichlids occupy territories between stones or roots in the calm water.

Tank Type: Central American Turquoise Stream

A slight current and clear water give a Central American Tank its radiance, which is effective only in fairly large tanks. The frequently metallic colors of the Central American cichlids and live-bearers are most impressive under very strong illumination (e.g., metal halide bulbs), but there should be some darker areas available around the perimeter of the tank. Here the less assertive species, such as *Thorichthys*, can find places to retreat in the shelter of projecting roots and brood, while the sprightly live-bearers settle in the open water. Central American fishes can't tolerate soft,

INFO

Tooth Carps or Live-bearers

Guppies, platies, and swordtails are part of the Poecilidae or the live-bearing tooth carps. In well-planted aquariums they bear numerous fry: After internal fertilization by the persistent males, the females give birth after a few weeks to well-developed live young, which are large enough to immediately eat dry food. Although the parents usually harm the fry, the throng quickly grows in the aquarium. So raise only as many fry as you will have accommodations for later on.

A brooding pair of firemouth cichlids in a Central American tank.

acidic water, so they are ideal "tap-water fishes" for areas with hard water.
General notes on care: Next to food rich in fiber and containing some green food, the most important requirement is the best possible water quality and effective filtering. A fine gravel substrate with river pebbles and well-waterlogged roots and some leaves. Mosquito larvae don't agree with *Thoricthys*.
Planting: Corkscrew *Vallisneria*, dwarf *Sagittaria*.

Suggested stocking No. 1 (40 × 14 × 14 in. / 100 × 40 × 40 cm)

- 10 red-tailed goodeids
- 10 (2/8) swordtails
- 10 platies or Blackbelly *Limia*
- 1/1 bristlenosed catfishes

Suggested stocking No. 2 (40 × 20 × 20 in. / 100 × 50 × 50 cm)

- 1/1 *Cryptheros* species
- 2/6 Humpbacked *Limia* or lampeye priapella
- 1/1 Bristlenosed Catfishes

Suggested stocking No. 3 (48 × 20 × 20 in. / 120 × 50 × 50 cm)

- 3/3 *Thorichthys* species
- 2/6 Humpbacked *Limia* or lampeye priapella
- 1/1 bristlenosed catfishes

Suggested stocking No. 4 (62 × 24 × 24 in. / 160 × 60 × 60 cm)

- 1/1 *Hypsophrys nicaraguense*
- 1/1 *Cryptoheros* species
- 15 swordtails
- 1/1 bristlenosed catfishes

Many Central American brooks and rivers have a high lime content.

Fish Profiles

The suggested stockings with these fishes appear on p. 101.

❶ Red-tailed Goodeid
Xenotoca eiseni; 2¾ in (7 cm)
Water type: 4–6; 64–79°F (18–26°C)
Minimum tank size: 14 gallons (50 l)

❷ Hump–backed Limia
Limia nigrofasciata; 2¾ in (7 cm)
Water type: 5–6; 75–80°F (24–27°C)
Minimum tank size: 28 gallons (100 l)

❸ Lampeye Priapella
Priapella intermedia; 2¾ in (7 cm)
Water type: 5–6; 77–82°F (25–28°C)
Minimum tank size: 41 gallons (150 l)

❹ Swordtail
Xiphophorus hellerii; 4¾ in (12 cm)
Water type: 4–6; 71–82°F (22–28°C)
Minimum tank size: 41 gallons (150 l)

❺ Platy
Xiphophorus maculatus; 2¼ in (6 cm)
Water type: 4–6; 70–77°F (22–25°C)
Minimum tank size: 14 gallons (50 l)

❻ Variable Platy
Xiphophorus variatus var.; 2¾ in (7 cm)
Water type: 4–6; 72–77°C (22–25°C)
Minimum tank size: 28 gallons (100 l)

❼ Firemouth Cichlid
Thorichthys meeki; 6 in (15 cm)
Water type: 4–6; 75–80°F (24–27°C)
Minimum tank size: 110 gallons (400 l)

❽ Thorichthys aureus
5 in (13 cm)
Water type: 5–6; 79–84°F (26–29°C)
Minimum tank size: 83 gallons (300 l)

❾ Macaw Cichlid, Parrot Cichlid
Hypsophrys nicaraguense; 10 in (25 cm)
Water type: 5–6; 75–80°F (24–27°C)
Minimum tank size: 138 gallons (500 l)

❿ Yellow Convict Cichlid
Cryptoheros nanoluteus; 4½ in (11 cm)
Water type: 5–6; 75–82°F (24–28°C)
Minimum tank size: 41 gallons (150 l)

⓫ T-bar Cichlid
Cryptoheros sajica; 4½ in (11 cm)
Water type: 5–6; 75–82°F (24–28°C)
Minimum tank size: 41 gallons (150 l)

⓬ Convict Cichlid
Cryptoheros nigrofasciatus; 6 in (15 cm)
Water type: 5–6; 73–80°F (23–27°C)
Minimum tank size: 69 gallons (250 l)

Popular Species for
Central American Tanks

A Lake Tanganyika Tank

Are you an aquarium hobbyists who is especially interested in the fascinating behaviors of fishes? Then this is the place for you. A Lake Tanganyika tank is impressive less for its special setup than for its fishes.

LAKE TANGANYIKA is one of the oldest lakes in the world. Nearly all animal and plant species that come from the lake live no place else and are thus endemic to it. Every depth area and every substrate type has its own distinctive community of living creatures. Cichlids from Lake Tanganyika are not always remarkable for their colors but for their unusual behavior and particularly elegant appearance. Most of the species favored for aquariums come from rocky areas. There are also some specialized inhabitants of sandy areas that should not be kept in small tanks along with the usually rougher rock dwellers. Lake Tanganyika cichlids often get along well with live-bearing tooth carps or rainbowfishes, for they have the same water-quality requirements.

Various Tank Types

Unaggressive inhabitants from various habitats (sandy, rocky, and open water areas) can be kept together in a large Tanganyika tank as long as it is large enough to provide each with its preferred habitat. In smaller tanks only one of these habitats should be simulated.

Accordingly, No. 1 tanks are pure sand tanks with a layer of sand 2 inches (6 cm) thick and empty shells from edible snails for *Neolamprologus multifasciatus*, which breeds no place else. If necessary, edges and open water can be occupied by *Vallisneria* and platies (from Central America). Suggested stocking No. 2 is a sand tank with a small rock structure in

INFO

Tanganyika Cichlids

Lake Tanganyika cichlids are distinguished by a broad spectrum of behaviors. There are mouth brooders and substrate brooders and species in which either the mother alone or both parents protect the eggs and fry. There are species that brood in cavities in the mud, empty snail shells, and holes in rocks, and others that leave the raising of their fairly large young to brooding catfishes. The cuckoo synodontis sneaks into the spawning sequence of maternal mouthbrooding cichlids, where it deposits its own eggs where they will be picked up—and subsequently brooded—by the unsuspecting female.

This large Tanganyika tank is occupied by
Cyphotilapia, *which grow to be large.*

which the striped julies can live. Suggested stocking No. 3 is a sand tank
with a large open water area and about
one-third of the tank as a cobble area,
where the Tanganyika clowns live. Suggested stocking No. 4 is a large tank
with a dominant sand area and a large
corner of rocks with vertical cracks in
which *Altolamprologus calvus* can live
and brood and get away from the catfish.

General notes on care: Regular, thorough water change, feeding with frozen
small crayfish (Cyclops) and high-
quality dry food containing spirulina.
Planting: Corkscrew *Vallisneria*, dwarf
Sagittaria.

Suggested stocking No. 1 (24 × 12 × 14 in. / 60 × 30 × 35 cm)

▸ 1/1 *Neolamprologus multifasciatus;* 6
  platies

Suggested stocking No. 2 (39 × 16 × 16 in. / 100 × 40 × 40 cm)

▸ 1/1 striped julies
▸ 1/1 *Neolamprologus multifasciatus*
▸ 10 platies or rainbowfishes

Suggested stocking No. 3 (48 × 20 × 20 in. / 120 × 50 × 50 cm)

▸ 1/1 *Xenotilapia papilio*
▸ 1/1 Tanganyika clowns
▸ 2/5 blue neons

Suggested stocking No. 4 (100 × 24 × 24 in. / 250 × 60 × 60 cm)

▸ 2/6 *Cyathorpharynx furcifer*
▸ 6 Cuckoo *Synodontis*
▸ 1/1 *Altolamprologus calvus*
▸ 1/1 elongated lemon cichlids

Popular Species for
Lake Tanganyika Tanks

Fish Profiles

The suggested stockings with these fishes can be found on p. 105.

❶ Elongated Lemon Cichlid
Neolamprologus longior; 4 inches (10 cm)
Water type: 5–6; 77–80°F (25–27°C)
Minimum tank size: 41 gallons (150 l)

❷ *Neolamprologus multifasciatus;*
2 inches (5 cm)
Water type: 5–6; 77–80°F (25–27°C)
Minimum tank size: 14 gallons (50 l)

❸ *Neolamprologus brevis;*
2½ inches (6 cm)
Water type: 5–6; 77–80°F (25–27°C)
Minimum tank size: 14 gallons (50 l)

❹ *Lamprologus ocellatus;*
2½ inches (6 cm)
Water type: 5–6; 77–80°F (25–27°C)
Minimum tank size: 14 gallons (50 l)

❺ Striped Julie or Convict Julie
Julidochromis regaini; 6 inches (15 cm)
Water type: 5–6; 77–80°F (25–27°C)
Minimum tank size: 41 gallons (150 l)

❻ *Altolamprologus calvus;*
5¾ inches (14 cm)
Water type: 5–6; 77–80°F (25–27°C)
Minimum tank size: 69 gallons (250 l)

❼ Blue Neon
Paracyprichromis nigripinnis 'Neon';
4½ inches (11 cm)
Water type: 5–6; 77–80°F (25–27°C)
Minimum tank size: 69 gallons (250 l)

❽ *Cyprichromis leptosoma;*
4¾ inches (12 cm)
Water type: 5–6; 77–80°F (25–27°C)
Minimum tank size: 96 gallons (300 l)

▲
Two Striped Julies in a natural setting in Lake Tanganyika.

❾ *Cyathopharynx furcifer;*
8¼ inches (21 cm)
Water type: 5–6; 77–80°F (25–27°C)
Minimum tank size: 193 gallons (700 l)

❿ *Xenotilapia papilio*
Water type: 5–6; 77–80°F (25–27°C)
Size: 3½ inches (9 cm)
Minimum tank size: 69 gallons (250 l)

⓫ Tanganyika Clown
Eretmodus cyanostictus; 4 inches (10 cm)
Water type: 5–6; 77–80°F (25–27°C)
Minimum tank size: 41 gallons (150 l)

⓬ Cuckoo Synodontis
Synodontis multipunctatus; 4¾ inches (12 cm)
Water type: 5–6; 77–80°F (25–27°C)
Minimum tank size: 165 gallons (600 l)

A Lake Malawi Tank

Distinguished by rock structures and a thin substratum, this is the character of a Lake Malawi aquarium. It is particularly effective in highlighting the marvelous colors of the courting male cichlids.

LIKE Lake Tanganyika, Lake Malawi is unique in its assembly of species. Here, in rocky, sandy, and open water zones, live only mouth-brooding cichlids from the *Haplochromis* group. Nearly all the species found in the lake are endemic. The rocky zone is inhabited by the comparatively aggressive and intensely colored "Mbuna" (rock cichlids). In contrast, the sandy and open water zones are populated mainly by the "chisawa-saw" and "utaka," which are noteworthy for their metallic colors and relatively calm temperament. The impressive colors have rightly brought the Malawi cichlids the name "freshwater coral fishes." In fact, the high concentration of fishes and the bright colors captivate even people who are not aquarium hobbyists. "Malawis" are among the most beloved aquarium fishes.

Various Tank Types

Malawi tanks should be structured strictly in accordance with the type of fish with which they will be stocked. Don't try to mix sand-dwelling cichlids, for the aggressive Mbunas are too domineering over the sand and open-water-living species. Mbuna tanks have large rock structures that can reach in layers right up to just below the water surface; ideally they are built to provide lots of opportunities for swimming through. Don't stack the rock structure right on the bottom of the aquarium or the substrate; instead, first put down a polystyrene underlay to avoid breaking the glass. Of course, the structures must not fall apart. The substrate may be thin and break after the stone structures are installed. Mbuna tanks should be brightly illuminated. Sand-dwelling and open-water-dwelling cichlids are kept in tanks with $2\frac{1}{2}$ inches (6 cm) of sand with a few fairly large stones, which serve to divide the tank into territories for the male cichlids.

INFO

Malawi Cichlids

If the Lake Tanganyika cichlids are the masters of caring for their young, the Lake Malawi cichlids are the color champions. The fabulous metallic, reflective, or gaudy colors of the courting males contrast with the usually unremarkable females. There is a reason for this, for the females carry the burden of mouth brooding. In choosing the most lavish males they want to be sure they are not dealing with a weakling, for only the strong have rich, beautiful colors.

Large Malawi tanks with Fossorochromis rostratus (in foreground) are a feast for the eyes.

General notes on care: A variety of foods including dry and frozen foods containing small crustaceans (Cyclops) and spirulina; regular, extensive water changes are particularly important. Filtering through a high-capacity outside filter. Lighting with a cold effect heightens the brilliance of the metallic colors. **Planting:** Corkscrew *Vallisneria*, dwarf *Sagittaria*.

Suggested stocking No. 1 (48 × 16 × 20 in. / 120 × 40 × 50 cm)

▶ 2/8 Demason's cichlids
▶ 8 *Labidochromis* sp. 'Yellow'
▶ 1/1 bristlenosed catfishes

Suggested stocking No. 2 (63 × 20 × 20 in. / 160 × 50 × 50 cm)

▶ 8 *Melanochromis auratus* or *M. johannii*

▶ 8 *Pseudotropheus lombardoi*
▶ 1/1 bristlenosed catfishes

Suggested stocking No. 3 (78 × 24 × 20 in. / 200 × 60 × 50 cm)

▶ 1/3 jacokfreibergi peacocks
▶ 1/3 red-fin kadango utakas
▶ 1/3 electric blue haps
▶ 1/1 bristlenosed catfishes

Suggested stocking No. 4 (100 × 24 × 24 in. / 250 × 60 × 60 cm)

▶ 5/8 *Placidochromis electra*
▶ 1/3 *Fossorochromis rostratus*
▶ 10 *Pseudotropheus socolofi*
▶ 10 siamese flying foxes

The red zebra in its natural habitat in Lake Malawi.

Fish Profiles

The suggested stockings with these fishes are given on p. 109.

❶ Peacock
Aulonocara jacobfreibergi; 5½ in (14 cm)
Water type: 5–6; 77–80°F (25–2°C)
Minimum tank size: 83 gallons (300 l)

❷ Red-fin Kadango Utaka
Copadichromis borleyi 'Kadango Red'; 5½ in (14 cm)
Water type: 5–6; 77–80°F (25–27°C)
Minimum tank size: 165 gallons (600 l)

❸ *Fossorochromis rostratus*
Size: 10 in (25 cm)
Water type: 5–6; 77–80°F (25–27°C)
Minimum tank size: 275 gallons (1000 l)

❹ Electric Blue Hap
Sciaenochromis fryeri; 8 in (20 cm)
Water type: 5–6; 77–80°F (25–27°C)
Minimum tank size: 110 gallons (400 l)

❺ *Placidochromis electra*
Size: 6¼ in (16 cm)
Water type: 5–6; 77–80°F (25–27°C)
Minimum tank size: 165 gallons (600 l)

❻ *Labidochromis* sp. 'Yellow'
Size: 4 in (10 cm)
Water type: 5–6; 77–80°F (25–27°C)
Minimum tank size: 69 gallons (250 l)

❼ *Melanochromis johannii*
Size: 5 in (12 cm)
Water type: 5–6; 77–80°F (25–27°C)
Minimum tank size: 69 gallons (250 l)

❽ *Melanochromis auratus*
Size: 4¾ in (11 cm)
Water type: 5–6; 77–80°F (25–27°C)
Minimum tank size: 83 gallons (300 l)

❾ *Pseudotropheus lonbardoi*
Size: 6 in (15 cm)
Water type: 5–6; 77–80°F (25–27°C)
Minimum tank size: 165 gallons (600 l)

❿ Red Zebra
Maylandia estherae; 4¾ in (11 cm)
Water type: 5–6; 77–80°F (25–27°C)
Minimum tank size: 83 gallons (300 l)

⓫ Powder Blue Cichlid
Pseudotropheus socolofi; 4¾ in (12 cm)
Water type: 5–6; 77–80°F (25–27°C)
Minimum tank size: 96 gallons (350 l)

⓬ Demason's Mbuna
Pseudotropheus demasoni; 3 in (8 cm)
Water type: 5–6; 77–80°F (25–27°C)
Minimum tank size: 69 gallons (250 l)

Popular Species for
Lake Malawi Tanks

A Brackish-Water Tank

Some fish species from brackish-water regions, such as moonies, also play a role in the aquarium hobby. Unfortunately, fishes that are adapted to salty water often have a short life in an aquarium because they are not cared for properly.

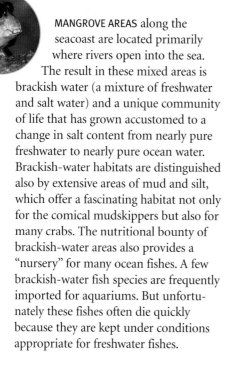

MANGROVE AREAS along the seacoast are located primarily where rivers open into the sea. The result in these mixed areas is brackish water (a mixture of freshwater and salt water) and a unique community of life that has grown accustomed to a change in salt content from nearly pure freshwater to nearly pure ocean water. Brackish-water habitats are distinguished also by extensive areas of mud and silt, which offer a fascinating habitat not only for the comical mudskippers but also for many crabs. The nutritional bounty of brackish-water areas also provides a "nursery" for many ocean fishes. A few brackish-water fish species are frequently imported for aquariums. But unfortunately these fishes often die quickly because they are kept under conditions appropriate for freshwater fishes.

Mangrove Tanks

Brackish-water tanks are most attractive when set up as mangrove tanks with tree roots and a sand bottom. I will provide several suggested stocking plans tailored specifically to the individual fish species. When properly cared for, these fishes needn't lead merely a sad, marginal existence. Suggested tank No. 1 is appropriate for small fishes that would be a concern in the company of other fish species. Every bumblebee goby needs its own miniature hiding place. Suggested tank No. 2 is a mini aqua-terrarium with a small section of land (sand piled up behind a root) and about 4 inches (10 cm) of water in the foreground. Lots of roots provide structure for this special tank for dwarf mudskippers.

Suggested tank No. 3 imitates a brightly illuminated brackish-water lagoon with a sand bottom, a few flat stones, and roots. Suggested tank No. 4 creates a home for the many brackish-

INFO

Brackish-Water Fishes

Brackish-water fishes belong to a broad spectrum of fish groups. Live-bearers, egg-laying tooth carps, and cichlids are predominantly freshwater groups that have a number of brackish-water representatives. However, there are many brackish-water inhabitants that belong to species groups that are distributed primarily in the ocean. But there are also fish groups whose distribution is restricted to brackish-water areas. These include scats, shark catfishes, moonies, and mudskippers. For aquarium life, all of them need a certain amount of salt, at least at times.

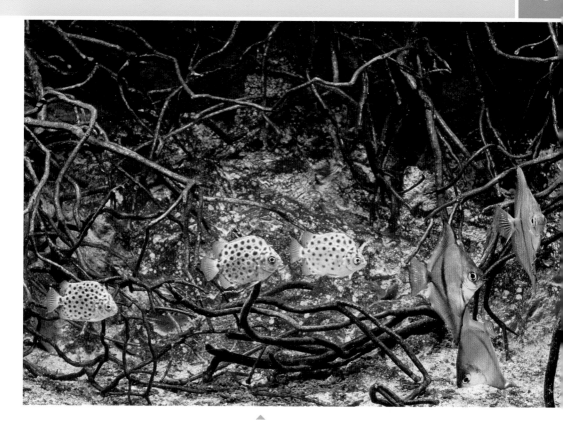

Scats and silver moonies, which rarely are given appropriate living conditions, in a large, realistic brackish-water tank.

water species that grow to be very large and require vitally important brackish water. Their tank is also set up with a sandy bottom, lots of room for free swimming, and large roots. A terrestrial component can be built up above the water.

General notes on care: A brackish-water tank "broken in" for an especially long time because the bacteria develop more slowly. It is especially important to offer these fish foods containing green food; feed gobies live *Artemia*. Adjust salt content using aquarium sea salt from a pet shop and an aerometer to a density of 1.002–1.007.

Planting: none

Suggested stocking No. 1 (24 × 12 × 14 in. / 60 × 30 × 35 cm)

▸ 25 bumblebee gobies or
▸ 4 figure-eight puffers

Suggested stocking No. 2 (24 × 12 × 14 in. / 60 × 30 × 35 cm)

▸ 2/4 Dwarf mudskippers

Suggested stocking No. 3 (48 × 20 × 20 in. / 120 × 50 × 50 cm)

▸ 2/2 orange chromides
▸ 20 black mollies or
▸ 3/8 sailfin mollies or
▸ 20 banded lampeyes

Suggested stocking no. 4 (126 × 28 × 20 in. / 320 × 70 × 50 cm)

▸ 8 shark catfishes
▸ 8 silver moonies
▸ 8 archerfishes
▸ 8 scats

Popular Species for
Brackish-Water Tanks

Fish Profiles

The suggested stockings with these fishes are given on p. 113.

❶ Black Molly
Poecilia sphenops var.; 3–4¾ in
(8–12 cm)
Water type: 5–7; 79–84°F (26–29°C)
Minimum tank size: 26.4 gallons (100 l)

❷ Banded Lampeye
Aplocheilichthys spilauchen; 2¾ in
(7 cm)
Water type: 7; 77–82°F (25–28°C)
Minimum tank size: 28 gallons (100 l)

❸ Sailfin Molly
Poecilia velifera; 6 in (15 cm)
Water type: 6–7; 77–82°F (25–28°C)
Minimum tank size: 106 gallons (400 l)

❹ Shark Catfish
Hexanematichthys seemanni; 18 in
(45 cm)
Water type: 7; 73–80°F (23–27°C)
Minimum tank size: 396 gallons (1500 l)

❺ Archer Fish
Toxotes cf. microlepis; 7 in (17 cm)
Water type: 5–7; 79–84°F (26–29°C)
Minimum tank size: 264 gallons (1000 l)

❻ Silver Moony
Monodactylus argenteus; 10 in (25 cm)
Water type: 7; 79–84°F (26–29°C)
Minimum tank size: 370 gallons (1400 l)

❼ Green or Spotted Scat
Scatophagus argus; 15 in (38 cm)
Water type: 7; 79–84°F (26–29°C)
Minimum tank size: 370 gallons (1400 l)

❽ Orange Chromide
Etroplus maculates; 3 in (8 cm)

▲
This mangrove is the perfect setting for Brackish-Water Fishes.

Water type: 6–7; 79–84°F (26–29°C)
Minimum tank size: 28 gallons (100 l)

❾ Bumblebee Goby
Brachygobius doriae; 1½ in (3.5 cm)
Water type: 5–7; 80–86°F (27–30°C)
Minimum tank size: 13 gallons (50 l)

❿ Dwarf Mudskipper
Periophthalmus novemradiatus;
1¾ in (5 cm)
Water type: 7; 73–80°F (23–27°C)
Minimum tank size: 13 gallons (50 l)

⓫ Figure-eight Puffer
Tetraodon biocellatus; 2½ in (6 cm)
Water type: 7; 43–45°F (6–7°C)
Minimum tank size: 13 gallons (50 l)

⓬ Hogchoker
Trinectes maculates; 8 in (20 cm)
Water type: 6–7; 43–45°F (6–7°C)
Minimum tank size: 93 gallons (350 l)

Frogs, Shrimps, Crabs, and Snails

It doesn't have to be all fishes. Other aquarium inhabitants also have their charms. Some of them even get along well with fishes. You too may find pleasure in this type of multicolored community.

African Dwarf Clawed Frogs

The strictly aquatic frogs of the genus *Hymenochirus* are always for sale in pet shops. They come from the shore regions of fairly small brooks and rivers in western and central Africa. These are comparatively undemanding, peaceable aquarium inhabitants that are happy with all frozen and live food species of the appropriate size: mosquito larvae, tubifex worms, water fleas, and even small strips of fish fillet. Socialization with fairly small fishes is entirely possible; you merely need to be sure that the fishes don't take the food away from the comparatively slow frogs. Also, particularly territorial fishes are not appropriate since the frogs don't learn to respect territorial boundaries of cichlids, for example. But guppies and killifishes are very good choices. Clawed frogs are great climbers, even along aquarium panes. The aquarium thus needs to be covered very tightly to eliminate any means of escape. A 24 inch (60 cm) aquarium with a small motor-driven inside filter, a thin gravel layer on the bottom, dim lighting, and plenty of plant growth, for example, Java moss

and crypts, plus a few dried red beech leaves (see p. 29), makes for a fine clawed frog home.

Shrimps and Crabs

In recent years colorful and comical crabs from freshwater and brackish water have turned into winners in aquariums. Many are ideal residents for a single species aquarium. Some species can also be kept in community aquariums along with fishes as long as you observe a few general rules: Offer them a variety of foods, for all species need a diet consisting of various types of live and frozen food (mosquito larvae, Cyclops, *Artemia* nauplii), dry, and green food. Mangrove crabs like cooked fish. African fan shrimps like to catch fine live and dry foods in the current, but they also accept other foods. A regular supply of dried beech leaves is important for molting (see p. 29). An adequate number of hiding places (at least one per creature, except for dwarf shrimps) such as a narrow bamboo tube. Never put them into a newly set-up aquarium. Most species are more sensitive than fishes to the chemical stress in the water, for example, from copper plumbing or stress brought on by previously administered fish medications. Just as with fishes, regular water changes and oxygen-rich aquarium water free from organic contaminants are important. Since these animals are good climbers, the cover plates absolutely must fit tightly together and be weighted down for larger species.

Crabs have a shell that doesn't grow, so they occasionally molt. The shed skin should remain in the aquarium for a while. Most species eat their own "discarded shirt" to recycle important nutrients. Depending on the species, freshwater crabs can be kept with other animals.

Snails

Snails can add to the variety of an aquarium. Some species have become naturalized as permanent components in the aquarium hobby, either because they are particularly handsome to look at, for example, apple snails (*Pomacea, Asolene,* and *Marisa* species), Malaysian cornucopia Snails with spines or knobs, and more recently, the attractive *Neratina natalensis*. Snails can also take over important tasks in an aquarium. Burrowing Malaysian cornucopia snails, for example, occupy the same niche in an aquarium substrate as night crawlers do in a garden: They aerate the substrate and make use of organic waste products. That way they encourage good plant growth. Other species, such as great ramshorn snails (*Planorbis, Planorbarius,* and *Planorbella*), pond snails (*Lymnaea* species), and even various apple snail species graze on the substrate for leftover food and thus help eliminate decaying matter. This helps

▲

The red-clawed mangrove crab needs a land component in a brackish-water aquarium.

the water quality. But in many cases they can also be a nuisance if they become too numerous—usually through overfeeding the fishes. When overabundant, they can do serious damage to live plants. Then they can be thinned out for esthetic reasons or removed (see p. 129). Snails either bear their young live or by depositing their lumplike egg clusters on plants or aquarium panes. Many species are hermaphroditic, so just one snail is all it takes to build up a new population.

❶ African Dwarf Clawed Frog
Hymenochirus boettgeri; 1½ inches (3.5 cm)
Water type: 2–5; 77–82°F (25–28°C)
Stocking: (24 × 12 × 14 in. / 60 × 30 × 35 cm): 6 African dwarf clawed frogs, 4/6 killifishes

There are many attractive species of freshwater lobsters from New Guinea.

❷ Red-clawed Mangrove Crab

Pseudoesarma moeshi; 2 inches (5 cm)
Water type: 6–7; 73–77°F (23–25°C)
Stocking: (24 × 12 × 14 in. (60 × 30 × 35 cm): 1/1 red-clawed mangrove crabs; small land portion important, for example, floating piece of cork bark; at least 4 inches (10 cm) of air between water surface and cover pane

❸ New Guinea Lobster or Zebra Crayfish

For example, zebra crab, *Cherax cf. papuanus;* 4⅜–8 inches (12–20 cm); Water type: 3–5, 70–77°F (20–25°C)
Stocking: (24 × 12 × 14 in. / 60 × 30 × 35 cm): 1/1 zebra crabs, 1/1 bristlenosed catfishes, 10 platies, plenty of food (also beech leaves); digs; this species requires lots of hiding places

❹ and ❺ Dwarf Crayfishes

Cajun dwarf crayfish, *Cambarellus shufeldtii;* 1½ inches (3 cm)
Mexican dwarf orange crayfish, *Cambarellus patzcuarensis;* 1¾ inches (4 cm)
Water type: 4–6; 61–73°F (16–23°C)
Stocking: (24 × 12 × 14 in. (60 × 30 × 35 cm): 15 animals, small bamboo tubes, Java moss beech leaves, humus; a variety of foods; will attack tank mates

❻ Blue Crayfish

Procambarus alleni; 4 inches (10 cm)
Living conditions as for New Guinea lobster ❸

❼ and ❽ Fan Shrimps

African fan shrimp, *Atya gabonensis;* 6 inches (15 cm)
Singapore shrimp, *Atyopsis molucensis;* 4 inches (10 cm)
Water type: 3–6; 73–79°F (23–26°C)
Stocking: (24 × 12 × 14 in. / 60 × 30 × 35 cm): single animal; likes current

❾ and ❿ Small Shrimp

Japanese glass shrimp, *Caridina cf. japonica;* 2¾ inches (7 cm)
Water type: 4–6, 59–82°F (15–28°C)
Crystal red shrimp, green dwarf shrimp; *Caridina* and *Neocaridina* species: ¾–1½ inches (2–4 cm)
Water type: 3–6; 70–77°F (20–25°C);
Stocking: (24 × 12 × 14 in. / 60 × 30 × 35 cm): 20 shrimps with 10 *Macrotocinclus hoppei;* keep in tank thickly planted with Java moss and Java fern; food granules, frozen Cyclops, algae, beech leaves

⓫ and ⓬ Golden Apple Snail

Pomacea bridgesi. Feed with zucchini and greens and dry food; feed animals individually or they will go hungry. *Neritina natalensis* or *Clypeolum latissimum, Neritidae* and *Clitho* can be kept in fairly hard water, but not for breeding.

Popular Species
in Profile

Reproduction in the Aquarium

It is entirely possible that a swarm of tiny fry will appear in a community aquarium. Every aquarium owner can intentionally breed fishes using simple means.

How Aquarium Fishes Reproduce

What really goes on when fishes reproduce? What's up when young fry suddenly are swimming around in a community tank? How can you easily raise a small number of fry? The answers are in this chapter.

THE APPROXIMATELY 25,000 FISH SPECIES have developed various and in some cases very spectacular ways of reproducing. Reproduction includes more than fertilization and spawning. Equally important are the courtship display for attracting a partner and creating the right mood, and in many cases, the demanding parental care of eggs and young that may go on for weeks. Many fish species even give birth to living fry, which, like mammals, are previously nourished in the female's body through a type of umbilical cord.

Place of Birth: Aquarium

You can observe the reproduction of your fishes in your aquarium because many species, when properly cared for, display their natural behaviors even in this restricted habitat. Some species even reproduce in a community tank with no encouragement from us; in other cases, special conditions for spawning, successful development of the eggs, and raising the fry must first be met. The breeding season of most fishes is coupled to the coming and going of the tropical seasons—the rainy and dry seasons and drought. In the aquarium, though, most species court and spawn throughout the year.

Courtship Display and Spawning

With most fish species the sexes choose their reproductive partners. In making their selection, they evaluate the potential partner according to criteria that are emphasized clearly in the mating display, the "courtship of the bride." Usually the males attract the unremarkable-looking females through extremely bright coloration and elaborate courtship behavior.

Many cichlids ▶ *(here a red zebra) are mouth brooders. Usually the females brood and release the fully developed young after several weeks.*

But there are also species in which it is mainly the female that does the courting. During the courtship in an aquarium, territories may be established that are vigorously defended against potential or real enemies and competitors temporarily or as long as the brooding continues. During this phase the behavior of these fished in the aquarium may become competitive and

a few species, such as platies, guppies, and swordtails, are live-bearers.

Eggs and Larvae

Tiny fish larvae, which look quite different from the adult parents, hatch from the eggs. Instead of individual fins they have a fin fringe and relatively large eyes and mouths. At first they have a yolk sac that sustains them during the first days of life. Only when nearly the entire yolk sac has been used up are the larvae

DID YOU KNOW THAT . . .

. . . many fishes have clever ways of reproducing?

Some favorite aquarium fishes from Lake Tanganyika have developed very particular reproduction strategies. For example, in order to escape the chore of brooding, the cuckoo synodontis (*Synodontis multipunctatus*) lays its eggs among those of mouth-brooding cichlids. Pairs deposit and fertilize their eggs with lightning speed at the same time as a spawning pair of mouth brooders. The female cichlid then takes the eggs of the catfish, which look like her own, into her mouth and incubates them there. But the baby catfishes hatch sooner than the cichlids, and they eat the developing cichlid embryos in the female cichlid's mouth. They then have the mouth, the protective "cave," all to themselves at the expense of the female's own young. After a few weeks of incubation the female cichlid releases several fully developed catfish fry to freedom.

problematic. With only a few exceptions, after successful courtship most females lay their eggs right in the open water (pelagic spawners) or on some sort of solid surface (substrate spawners). At that time or shortly thereafter, the eggs are fertilized by the male. Only

of most fishes capable of swimming in open water and taking in nutrients. From then on they grow continually as long as they get enough food. The eggs and larvae of most species that do not provide care for the brood are significantly smaller and more numerous than the ones produced by species that care

You need to have foster homes or plenty of room for your fish offspring.
Be sure to make provisions for this in advance.

for their young or give birth live. Unless very small food is provided, rearing fry of these species is rarely successful because of their small mouths.

The fry of the species that care for the brood, for example, cichlids, are, like those of live-bearers, quite large and generally are fairly easy to raise.

Caring for the Young

Quite a number of aquarium fishes display their entire behavior repertory in the aquarium. One of the most fascinating observations that are possible in an aquarium is certainly watching the often elaborate caring for the brood, which can vary greatly from one fish group to the next.

Open and cavity brooders: Many cichlids and gobies lay their eggs on an open substrate (open brooders) or in a cave (cavity brooders). Then they are fanned, cleaned, and guarded either by the male (gobies) or the females (some cichlids), or both partners (many cichlids). Later on cichlids also take good care of the larvae and free-swimming fry.

Mouth brooders: Some cichlids, labyrinth fishes, and others are mouth brooders. Males, females, or both incubate the larvae and fry in their mouths for several days or weeks. When the fry are fairly large, with many species they are let out of the mouth temporarily to eat. But the little ones return to the parent's mouth for shelter. Many fish species even feed their young inside the mouth.

Foam nest: The males of many labyrinth fishes build a foam nest on the surface of the water. There the females lay their eggs. The foam nest is defended until hatching and/or the time when the larvae can swim on their own. Most species are very territorial, especially during the brooding phase, for the survival of the fry is ensured only if the young stay in a "safety zone" where they can find adequate food without being threatened by enemies. This brood territory is defended aggressively against all aquarium inhabitants and against fishes with which the "bride and groom" have previously lived peacefully. During this phase it may be necessary

_____

The cuckoo syndontis slips its eggs in among those of mouth-brooding cichlids.

▶ **1** **Before successful** pairing there very frequently are major quarrels—as shown here with a pair of mouth-fighting *Parachromis loisellei.*

▶ **2** **With many mouth brooders** (here *Siaenochromis*) the eggs are first fertilized in the mouth of the female.

▶ **3** **With many species** caring for the young falls to both parents, which like a devoted couple, lead the brood to food and defend them vehemently if necessary.

to accommodate stressed fishes separately or separate the incubating parents from the rest of the inhabitants with a glass partition.

Breeding and Rearing Made Easy

Sometimes offspring suddenly appear in a holding or community tank. With brooding species, such as cichlids, the parents defend a swarm of tiny fry in their brood territory and help with the rearing in the holding tank. Such fry are often relatively large and robust, for otherwise they never would have managed to swim free in the holding tank. You can try to raise them in the tank with a few little tricks.

▶ Several time a day give them dry food for young fishes or *Artemia* nauplii (see p. 127), which you can deposit near the fry using something like a basting syringe, so that the food for the fry doesn't permeate the whole tank.

▶ Change the water more frequently, about one-third of the aquarium water twice a week, because the larger quantity of food places a greater strain on the aquarium water.

▶ Isolate some fry in what's known as a spawning box, which should be suspended in the holding tank and equiped with a couple of floating plant stems (e.g., Hornwort). Place the babies in the spawning box with a glass or a fine net so that they remain under water. It's easier to feed a small number of fishes in the box—but such spawning boxes are too small for rearing the brood to more than about a $\frac{1}{2}$ (1.5 cm) in body length; then the rearing should take place in a nursery tank (see below).

Note: Always raise only as many fry as you need to ensure the stocking of your own aquarium or for which you have takers in your circle of acquaintances. There is no sense in raising a large quantity of fry for which you have no

room or no takers, and it borders on cruelty to animals.

The Nursery Tank

For raising a small number of larvae or fry that you have rescued from the community tank, you should set up a special easy-to-clean nursery tank with water from the holding tank. To raise about 20 fry to a size of about $\frac{3}{4}$–$1\frac{1}{4}$ inches (2–3 cm) you should use a small glass aquarium (about 7 gallons (25 l); 16 × 10 × 10 in. / 40 × 25 × 25 cm) set up with an air-driven inside filter that has already been broken in for some time in another tank. In addition, depending on the fish species, you should add a few sprouting stem plants, Java moss, or small hiding places (sections of plastic hose, birch leaves), for even fry are often territorial and want to hide from one another. Do not use substrate so that you can easily remove leftover food and excrement. You must do this carefully by vacuuming only

the floor with an air hose. Apple or *Planorbis* snails can complete the tank because they eat leftover food. Frequent, regular, partial water changes are especially important—preferably replace one-third of the aquarium water with conditioned water every day or two.

Raising *Artemia* Nauplii

Freshly hatched *Artemia* nauplii, the larvae of small swimming crustaceans, are a nutritious food for young and adult fishes.

Hatching *Artemia* Eggs: Start by putting an iodine-free salt solution (one heaping tablespoon of salt to 1 quart/liter of water) into an empty liter wine bottle. Add a $\frac{1}{2}$ teaspoon full of *Artemia* eggs from a pet shop. Connect an air hose attached to an aeration tube about 1 foot (30 cm) long to an aquarium aeration pump so that the hose reaches the bottom of the bottle and the air keeps the eggs in motion (alternatively, buy an *Artemia* raising kit from the pet shop). Place the bottle in a

◀ *Dwarf cichlids like this* Microgeophagus altispinosca *spend weeks caring for their larvae and fry.*

warm location. After about 36–48 hours the nauplii hatch and can be fed. Shut off the air pump to feed them. The eggshells rise to the top, and the reddish nauplii collect under them. They can be sucked up with the air hose and poured into a special *Artemia* strainer. Rinse them briefly in soft water and put the red mass right into the aquarium or the spawning box using a teaspoon. Covered with a little salt water, *Artemia* nauplii keep for several hours in a refrigerator so that you can get two meals from one "harvest." It's a good idea to use two or three bottles in shifts.

MY PET

Influencing fish behavior

By using a mirror or a photo, you can trigger interesting behaviors in the holding tank among many territorial and actively reproducing fishes, such as fighting fishes—especially if there is no partner or competitor in the tank.

The test begins:

Take a pocket mirror and hold it in front of, say, a male fighting fish. The fish will spread its fins, lower its jaw, intensify its colors, and display in front of the supposed opponent. In a similar experiment you can use the photo of a female fighting fish to trigger the courtship display in a male. The picture acts as a substitute for the male. What do you observe?

My test results:

What to Do When There Are Problems

Most problems that arise in an aquarium are the result of a
lack of information. And yet even the most experienced aquarist
may be confronted with problems.

Emergency Help

An aquarium is a small slice of nature. It's precisely this spatial restriction that makes the aquarium habitat susceptible to disturbances. This chapter will show you how to deal with the most common problems.

AN AQUARIUM is more than water and a collection of fishes; it's a complex community of life that is the product of the interaction of various fish and plant species, various accessories, water values, and foods. The functioning of this interplay can be regulated by providing the right basic conditions, and yet it's not always entirely controllable. Even the pros can have problems, for example, when one aquarium is operating well but another, with the same basic conditions, simply doesn't work. But many problems can be solved through careful consideration of the species-specific care requirements.

Snail Infestation

Situation: Small snails are reproducing in excess and are stuck all over the aquarium.
Possible causes: You may have introduced snail eggs (in the form of a lumpy mass with dark spots sometimes visible on the aquarium glass) on aquatic plants or live food. The snails have reproduced prolifically because they have encountered especially favorable conditions (lots of leftovers food) and no enemies.

What you can do: Don't put chemical snail preparations into the operating aquarium. Snails are not harmful, except perhaps when gnawing on water plants. You can try to limit the snail nuisance, but you will never succeed in totally eliminating it. But that's not even necessary. It's best to set up a home-made snail trap: Place a saucer with a food tablet on it inside the aquarium and cover it with an empty yogurt container with holes in it. (The snails will be able to get through, but not the fishes. The snails are attracted and will collect overnight in the yogurt container and can be removed. Pet shops

A few snails are welcome in most aquariums, but with an excess of food from overfeeding the fishes, there can be massive reproduction. ▶

also sell plastic snail traps. Snail-eating fishes may also help. This requires a thorough matching of the socialization and care requirements, however. Snail-eating fishes include the pufferfish, clown loach, and *Neolamprologus multifasciatus*. Many pufferfish species and clown loaches become very large and are aggressive toward fishes of other species.

Blue-green Algae Infestation

Situation: Especially in the first few weeks and months after setting up the aquarium, there is a continuous dark-green or blue-green "carpet" of grimy algae on both the substrate and the accessories and plants. As you do your aquarium chores you may notice a musty smell.

Cause: Your aquarium is suffering from a blue-green algae infestation. Blue-green algae really are not algae but rather bacteria that can reproduce at top speed—although it's not always clear why.

What you can do: Suck up all algae coatings with a large hose when you are doing a major water change. Keep the aquarium as dark as possible and put in an oxygen releaser (see p. 24). Feed sparingly and repeat the suction process (including a major water change) as soon as a new algae carpet begins to appear. If you have a well-planted aquarium with plants that need lots of

1 **With killifishes** (here *Fundulopanchax gardneri*) and many other species the males compete with imposing and aggressive displays for the favor of and access to the females.

2 **With species that** take care of their brood, the aggressiveness of the parents toward other species increases further when the fry begin to swim. It may become necessary to remove some of the fishes.

Dwarf royal farlowellas are sensitive indicators of deteriorating water quality. ▶

light, put in a fairly large quantity of fast-growing water plants, such as Hornwort, and keep providing normal illumination. Check the nitrite and nitrate water values at intervals of several days and keep them low through water changes. Only after everything else has failed, put in a special anti-blue-green-algae preparation from the pet shop. Usually the water conditions in an area unfriendly to blue-green algae stabilize after a few weeks, and the algae disappear as inexplicably as they appeared. You can encourage stabilization of the water values through temporary zeolite filtering (see p. 23).

The Fishes Are Not Doing Well

Situation: After a water change the fishes are breathing heavily, and often they hang close under the surface of the water. A check of the pH yields a value above 7.

Possible causes: Ammonia poisoning after a sudden pH spike higher than 7. Ammonia is a poison that results from the breakdown of biological waste products, but normally it is converted to nitrate in several steps by filter bacteria. If the most recent water change was some time ago, if the tank is over-populated, or if for other reasons it has accumulated excessive biological waste that the bacteria cannot completely process (because the filter capacity is inadequate), at pH levels below 7 the relatively nonpoisonous intermediate product ammonium will be the result.

If the pH value rises above 7 through a water change with alkaline (tap) water, the ammonium will turn into poisonous ammonia and produce symptoms of poisoning in the fishes.

What you can do: Carefully change 90 percent of the aquarium water to eliminate the poisonous waste products nearly completely from the aquarium. Clean the filter and vacuum the substrate. With demanding fishes that can't tolerate massive water changes, you can slowly (!) reduce the pH level to below 7 by using pH reducers from the pet shop and continually checking the pH level. This allows you to convert the ammonia back to ammonium but not to remove it. So over several days perform partial water changes with pre-prepared water (see p. 57). Zeolite filtering (according to the directions)

We Want to Take a Vacation...

Our daughter has an aquarium. We would like to go on vacation with her for 3 weeks. However, she refuses to leave the aquarium. How can we convince her that the fishes will be well cared for if we go away together?

IT'S BEST TO discuss with your daughter the possibility of getting someone to take care of the fishes for 3 weeks. Of course if you are going to be gone longer you will have to make arrangements for regular feeding, checking the technical equipment, and possibly even changing the water. You thus need a competent, reliable person to take over the care of your aquarium.

A vacation substitute

About 2 weeks before vacation you should start to introduce your vacation replacement to the aquarium to make sure that all the chores are understood and are performed together once. This is also a good time to see if all the life support equipment is working perfectly and flawlessly while there is still time to get replacements and check them out. This is especially true for automatic feeders in case a replacement is needed during your absence. In order to create optimum conditions, you should prepare the aquarium before your vacation: 2 days before your departure change 50 percent of the aquarium water. Keep enough water on hand in case a water change is needed. Lay in a good supply of food. Load an automatic feeder for the first week if your fishes eat dry food (food should not be kept for a longer time in an automatic feeder). Set the food rations that your vacation replacement should give the fishes to avoid inadvertent overfeeding and consequent stress on the water. In order to address any questions that may arise, exchange telephone numbers or e-mail addresses before the vacation. Talk in advance about possible problems (e.g., the filter stops working, the fishes get sick, there is a dead fish in the aquarium).

Fasting time

By the way, you can leave an aquarium that has been running well to date for up to a week without attention and feeding, for healthy adult fishes at least $1^{1}/_{2}$ inches (4 cm) long can easily withstand a week's fasting. And don't use any controlled-release food, because the ingredients can put a real strain on the water if the fishes don't eat it.

also helps to keep the ammonium/ammonia levels low and can be used as a preventive measure.

The Nitrate Level Won't Go Down

Situation: You have checked the nitrate level before and right after changing the water in your aquarium and detect little or no improvement. Usually you also have algae problems. In checking the tap water, you discover nitrate levels well above 20 mg/liter, sometimes above 50 mg/liter.

Cause: Your tap water is already contaminated with nitrate and perhaps also with other toxins (phosphates and pesticides).

What you can do: Set up a reverse-osmosis device (available at pet shops) for preparing water. It produces nearly distilled water plus leftover water that you can use for such purposes as watering flowers. Reverse-osmosis water is also mostly free of toxic substances, and even from hardness builders, so it is usable as aquarium water only with fishes adapted to very soft water (water type 1). Depending on the care requirements of the fishes, you normally add salt (from the pet shop) to the reverse-osmosis water to obtain the most appropriate type of water.

Large fishes must be fed with fairly large quantities of food, which can place a major strain on the water.

Questions about
Fish-keeping Problems

? **At a the gardening center I bought some silver sharks, giant catfishes, and shark catfishes. Even though I was told that the fishes would fit in my 3-foot (1-meter) tank, they have grown very large, some over 8 inches (20 cm). Now what should I do?**

When you bought your fishes, you didn't have enough information, and you were given some bad advice. Try to give your fishes away to other aquarists you know who have larger tanks. If you were given incorrect advice, responsible pet shop owners will take the fishes back and find customers with appropriate accommodations for them. You can also try to give your fishes away to responsible parties by searching on special aquarium sites on the Internet. If you can't locate anyone who wants to adopt the fishes, you should get a larger aquarium to provide them with a more appropriate habitat.

? **A white, crusty coating has formed on the water plants. The pH level has gone above 8. What is the cause?**

The water plants are suffering from a deficiency in the important plant nutrient carbon dioxide. This happens with particular frequency in aquarium water with elevated carbonate hardness because there is little carbon dioxide for the plants in carbonate hard water (e.g., water types 5–6). To compensate for the lack of carbon dioxide, the plants make use of the carbon contained in the carbonate hardness builders. In the process a harmful coating of lime forms on the leaves and the pH level goes up. The only remedy involves adding carbonate-poor water (e.g., reverse-osmosis water) and/or carbon dioxide fertilizer. There are several other procedures—get some advice from your pet shop on which method makes sense for your tank size, water values, and financial means.

? **Light-green deposits of thick, short or fairly long, stringy algae are forming everywhere in the aquarium. However, no greasy coating forms. What should I do about this?**

In most cases the nutrient content in the aquarium water is too high because of infrequent water changes, crowding with fishes, or excessive feeding. Sometimes an imbalance among illumination, fertilization, and aquatic plant growth is the culprit. Water plants should be fertilized only in proportion to the amount of nutrients they require. A slightly green algae growth, in contrast to excessive stringy or blue-green algae, is not harmful but rather often is an indication of good water conditions. With excessive growth you may initially reduce the excessive nutrient strain in the water through water changes. Zeolite filtering also decreases the amount of organic metabolic products. String algae can be

wound up on a small stick and removed. Fishes that eat green algae, especially bristlenosed catfishes for fairly large aquariums and *Otocinclus* sp. or flying foxes for smaller tanks, can help keep the green algae down. Japanese glass shrimp also like to eat string algae. But in utilizing living algae eaters, remember that they need green food after they have annihilated the algae. Also, not all species can be housed successfully with one another. Get the information you need about community compatibility, for example, from the suggested stockings on pp. 72–119.

❓ In my aquarium the larger cichlid male chases the smaller female. How can I protect the female?

There are frequent problems even with mating pairs of cichlids (and many other fishes) when they have to live in a restricted space. In the wild, the fishes can get away from one another, but that's not possible in an aquarium. If the selected partners don't get along despite being of the same species, for reasons of individual preferences or if they have had a falling out over a failed brood or something similar, the dominant fish can inflict serious injury on the weaker one—especially when there is no opportunity for retreat. There are several ways to start or rekindle a pairing. One possibility is to separate the bickerers with a pane of glass so they can continue to see each other. When they are fed well, the two often will get used to each other again, and after a while—at least on a probationary basis—they can be allowed back together. An alternative in somewhat larger tanks is to provide a large number of additional hiding places, preferably in which the smaller fish can fit but not the larger one. Sections of PVC pipe are especially good for this; they can be hung near the water surface with plastic-coated wire. The larger fish often will not search there.

The smaller one can retreat there in safety and still seek the goodwill of the larger one. The bond will usually reestablish itself after a time.

Fish or Aquarium Sitter

Do you want to go away on vacation and have a pet sitter take care of your aquarium? Here you can write down everything that your sitter needs to know. That way your fishes get the best possible care and you can enjoy your vacation to the fullest.

Type of aquarium:

Type of filter and filter material:

Lighting:

What fishes are in the aquarium?

How many fishes are there in the aquarium?

Types of food:

How often to feed:

How much to feed:

What to look for in checking the tank:

Frequency of water changes:

Where to get the water for the partial water

change:

Regularly check these water values:

Additional care:

If there is a dead fish in the tank:

If the aquarium springs a leak:

Emergency address:

My vacation address and phone number:

INDEX

ASSOCIATIONS/ CLUBS

American Killifish Association
www.aka.org

American Cichlid Association
P.O. Box 5351
Naperville, IL
60567-5351

Aquatic Gardeners Association
83 Cathcart St.
London, Ontario
Canada N6L 3L9

International Betta Congress
923 Wadsworth St.
Syracuse, NY
13208-2419

North American Discus Society
6939 Justin Drive
Mississauga, Ontario
Canada, L4T 1M4

American Livebearer Association
Timothy J. Brady,
Membership Chairman
5 Zerbe Street
Cressona, PA
17929-1513
tjbrady@fast.net

Federation of American Aquarium Societies (FAAS)
Hedy Padgett
(Membership Chair)
4816 E. 64th Street
Indianapolis, IN
46220-4728

Local Aquarium Clubs

Virtually every town and city in the United States has at least one (often more than one) aquarium club. For details, refer to the relevant local telephone directory or search the Internet.
Questions about all aquarium-related topics (fish keeping, water plants, fish diseases, aquarium equipment, basic water chemistry, etc.) can be directed to your local aquarium or specialist pet shop staff. There are also numerous aquarium forum sites available on the Internet that deal with these topics.

Aquarium insurance

For third-party, liability, and personal injury insurance contact the major insurance companies in your area.

Magazine and Journals

Tropical Fish Hobbyist
TFH Publications, Inc.
Neptune, NJ

Freshwater & Marine Aquarium (FAMA)

Aquarium Magazine

Practical Fish Keeping (UK)

Aquarist and Pond Keeper (UK)

Books

Lambert, Derek. *The Aquarium Fish Handbook.* Hauppauge, NY: Barron's Educational Series, Inc., 2004.

Hiscock, Peter. *Aquarium Designs Inspired by Nature.* Hauppauge, NY: Barron's Educational Series, Inc., 2003.

Gula, Wolfgang. *Plants for Your Aquarium.* Hauppauge, NY: Barron's Educational Series, Inc., 2002.

Sanford, Gina. *The Tropical Aquarium.* Hauppauge, NY: Barron's Educational Series, Inc., 2004.

Herndal, Jay F. *Aquarium Fish Breeding.* Hauppauge, NY: Barron's Educational Series, Inc., 2003.

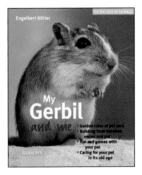

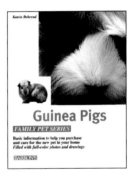

Photo Credits

Anders: 119-1; Aquapress: 97, 105, 113; Bork: 78, 82-12, 83, 95-5, cover 5 left, cover 6 left; Buescher: 15, 105, 106-3, 106-10, 107; Eheim-Aquaistik: 19-1; Giel: 62, 132; Giesemann-Aquaristik: 19-2; Hartl: 51, 64, 69, 71 left, 71 right, 74, 75, 79-2, 95-3, 95-6, 96, 98-6, 98-10, 102-12, 114-5, cover 3 middle; Hecker: 31, 35 bottom, 119-2; Kahl: 1, 4, 20, 28-3, 30, 34 top, 34 bottom middle, 34 bottom, 35 top, 35 top middle, 45, 47-1, 47-2, 47-3, 47-4, 56, 65, 72, 77 new, 79-4, 80. 81. 82-4, 82-5, 92-6, 85, 87-2, 87-3, 88, 89, 90, 90-4, 90-5, 90-9, 90-10, 92, 95-7, 95-11, 95-12, 103-1, 103-2, 106-2, 106-6, 109, 114-1, 114-3, 114-7, 114-9, 116, 119-5, 119-6, 119-8, 119-10, cover 1, cover 4 top left, cover 4 top right, cover 4 bottom left, cover 4 bottom right, cover 5 right, cover 6 right,; Kölle: 66 bottom; Koslowski: 2 top, 22, 24, 25 left, 25 right, 28-1, 33, 50-2, 60-1, 66 top right, 68-2, 71 middle, 82-3, 82-7, 82-10, 87-1, 87-6, 87-9, 87-11, 90-6, 90-11, 95-8, 98-12, 106-5, 106-11, 114-2, 117, 119-7, 119-9, 130 right, 131; Lamboj: 79-11, 87-8, 95-4, 98-7, 103-3, 106-1, 114-6, 120, 128; Linke: 7, 26, 28-2, 36, 37, 40, 79-1, 82-9, 86, 90-1, 94; Lucas: 2 bottom, 12, 48, 50-1, 59, 76, 79-9, 79-10, 79-12, 84, 87-4, 87-5, 90-12, 95-2, 119-11, 119-12, 121, cover 7; Nieuwenhuizen: 8, 79-7, 79-8, 87-7, 90-7, 90-8, 95-9, 103-5, 126, 129, cover 8; Peither: 5, 17, 39, 95-10, 114-11, 123, cover 2 bottom, cover 3 top; Reinhard: 115; Schliewen: 43, 130 left; Schmida: 98-2, 98-3, 98-8, 99; Schmidbauer: 16, 52, 54, 60-3, 91, 102, 103-6, 112, 114-10, cover 3 top; Spreinat: 10, 19-3, 21, 42-1, 42-2, 53, 57, 60-2, 63, 66 to left, 66 middle, 68-1, 87-12, 98-4, 100, 103-9, 106-8, 108, 110, 111-2, 111-3, 111-4, 111-5, 111-6, 111-7, 111-8, 111-9, 111-10, 111-11, 111-12, 119-4, 133, 135 left, 135 middle, 135 right; Staeck: 6, 27, 44, 49, 73, 79-5, 79-6, 98-1, 103-7, 106-12, 111-1, 114-8, 124, 125 left, 125 right, Weidner: 82-8; Werner: 9, 13 top, 13 bottom, 29, 38 79-3, 82-11, 87-10, 93, 98-9, 101, 103-4, 103-8, 103-10, 103-11, 114-12, 118, 119-3, 122, cover 2 top; Zurlo: 82-2, 95-1, 98-11, 106-4, 106-7, 106-9, 114-4

Editing: Christine Axmann, Gabriele Linke-Grün
Photo Editor: Adriane Andreas
Cover Design: Independent Media Design
Inside Layout: Independent Media Design
Typesetting: Christopher Hammond
Production: Suzanne Mühldorfer
Reproduction: Fotolito Longo, Bozen
Printing and Binding: Druckhaus Kaufmann, Lahr
Translated from German by: Eric A. Bye, M.A.

G|U

First edition for the United States, its territories and dependencies and Canada published in 2008 by Barron's Educational Series, Inc.

German edition by: Ulrich Schliewen

Published originally under the title *mein Aquarium*, in the series *mein Heimtier* © 2006 by Gräfe and Unzer Verlag GmbH, München

All inquiries should be addressed to:
Barron's Educational Series, Inc.
250 Wireless Blvd.
Hauppauge, NY 11788
www.barronseduc.com

ISBN-13: 978-0-7641-3798-3
ISBN-10: 0-7641-3798-0
Library of Congress Cataloging-in-Publication Data

Schliewen, Ulrich.
  [Mein Aquarium. English]
  My aquarium / Ulrich Schliewen. – 1st ed.
    p. cm.—(My pet)
  Includes index.
  ISBN-13: 978-0-7641-3798-3 (alk. paper)
  ISBN-10: 0-7641-3798-0 (alk. paper)
 1. Aquariums. 2. Aquarium fishes. 3. Aquarium plants. I. Title.

SF457.3.S36513 2008
639.34—dc22

2007040905

Printed in China

9 8 7 6 5 4 3 2